The Bad
and
Downright Ugly
of the
German-Russian
Volga Colonies

D. Philipp Kaiser

First Dedication

This book, as well as any future books I may write, is dedicated to the memory of my recently passed beloved and treasured wife,

BETTY MAY KAISER

Her caring love, constant companionship, unwavering support, and unlimited patience inspired and guided me as we walked our Lord's path together, both as Best Friends for over 45 years, and as one as Man and Wife for over 40 years.

My Betty, my one and only love, still and always. My eternal thanks… Soon we will meet again.

Second Dedication

This book is dedicated to my Great Grandfather Johann Conrad (Red) Simon. His wise decision to move his family to the United States in 1907 saved them from going through the horror of the famines and deportation. After his wife Maria Christina died, Red returned to his Volga River. He remained there and did not escape the horrors that the German-Russian people of the Volga endured. He was never heard of again.

Johann Conrad (Red) Simon

A Prayer for Genealogists

*Lord, help me dig into the past and sift the
sands of time,
That I might find the roots that made this family
tree mine.
Lord, help me trace the ancient roads on which
my fathers trod,
And led them through so many lands to find our
present sod.*

*Lord, help me find an ancient book, or dusty
manuscript,
That's safely hidden now away in some
forgotten crypt.
Lord, let it bridge the gap that haunts my soul
when I can't find,
The missing link between some name that ends
the same as mine.*

Curtis Woods

Preface

This book attempts to identify the hardships that the German-Russian colonists endured and overcame in the Volga Colonies. The First Chapter covers their emigration to the Volga Colonies. The Second Chapter covers the Shock and Disappointment, Death Rate, Wild Weather, Sickness, and Food Shortages that they endured. Chapter 3 is about Tsarina Catherine the Great and her "promises." Chapter 4 covers the Robber Bands and Nomadic Tribes, and their terrorizing of the colonies. The tale of Emelian Pugachev is in Chapter 5. Chapter 6 covers Lenin and the Red Guards, and the Rebellion in Warenburg. Chapter 7 is the last chapter and is all about Famine in Germany and the Volga Colonies. Following that is a Summary, a Bibliography and Endnotes.

This book is one in a series of books on the German-Russians of the Volga Colonies. For more information on the Volga Colonies, some of my other books are:

"Origin & Ancestors Families Karle & Kaiser of the German-Russian Volga Colonies"

"Moscow's Final Solution: The Genocide of the German-Russian Volga Colonies"

"Emigration to and from the German-Russian Volga Colonies"

For information on this and other books I have written on a variety of topics including more on the German-Russian Volga Colonies, historical novels, Watercolor quilts, basic electrical troubleshooting, sewing machine maintenance, the original Sewhandy sewing machine, and the SINGER Model 221 Featherweight.... Please visit my websites at

www.DarrelKaiserBooks.com
www.Volga-Germans.com

Your comments and/or submissions to improve this book are always appreciated. Discussions as to the validity of my theories and assumptions are welcome. Submission of copies of photographs or documents that are applicable to the subject is encouraged, and credit will be given in the next edition.

Email me with any and all comments or questions at

Dar-Bet@att.net

I sincerely hope you find this book interesting and educational!

Table of Contents

Chapter 1
Emigration

The emigration to Russia for the German Colonists heading for the Volga Colonies was long and difficult. They had to pack up what little they could carry and travel by river and overland to the port city of Lübeck on the northeastern coast of Germany. They might also have gone west to the port city of Rotterdam on the Netherland coast.

Emigration Itinerary

1) Central Germany overland or by river either North to Hannover and then Lubeck, or West to Rotterdam

2) Travel the NorthSea by packet ship from Rotterdam to the Baltic Sea, or from Lubeck to the Baltic Sea, and then North to St Petersburg

3) Process in Russia

Path of Emigration to Lübeck and St Petersburg [1]

Once in Lübeck, the colonists had to wait a long time due to the large crowds. The wealthier emigrants were given housing by Commissioner Schmidt in one of the nearby homes, and probably lived comfortably.[2] Most of my ancestors were probably very poor, and had to live in the large crowded and smelly barracks.

These were originally the "Wulf" warehouses located near the city or other warehouses near the Holstein Bridge. They were buildings without stoves, drafty, and with straw on the floor,[3] near the harbor. These buildings were overcrowded, filthy, disease spreading, and rodent infested. There were also many undesirables waiting to exploit of the colonists they could.[4]

The response to Catherine the Greats' Manifesto was most obvious in Lübeck. Thousands waited there to leave as early as 1765. While waiting, the colonists received daily allowances dependant on gender and age. Men received eight, women 5, children 3, and infants 1 schilling a day. Some men were given temporary titles such as "sheriff" and "foreman" for distributing this money and rations.

The stay in the cities was at times long because of weather and climatic conditions, frozen rivers, no money, and no room on ships. During these extended stays there were baptisms and weddings, and lucky for us many of the records point to the regions of origin. These were held at the various gathering places.

The massive influx of people put a great strain on the resources of Lübeck. For a while, the city leaders opposed the housing of so many colonists. Eventually, the city leaders realized that all this movement brought lots of money into the city, and they became very supportive. In fact, the city authorities even aided the Recruiter agents and Russian enrollers in forcing any colonists that decided to not go to Russia to live up to their contracts.[5]

At Rotterdam, it was probably not as crowded, but they still would have had to wait until it was their time to board a ship for the 1,500-mile trip over the North Sea and across the Baltic Sea to the Russian port city of St. Petersburg.

Next Stop: Kronstadt, Russia

They left on Hanseatic or English ships, or small Russian packet ships to cross the Baltic Sea. A picture of a packet ships is on the right.[6] Some of the sailing vessels used could transport 280 people at a time; some were limited to much less.

Once on board, the settlers had a voyage of nine to 11 days to cover about 450 miles ahead of them. In poor weather, the voyage might take up to six weeks with food and water becoming scarce. There were also Captains who lengthened the trip unnecessarily to force the colonists to spend their travel money entirely on rations.[7]

One emigrant named Bernhard Ludwig von Platen waited two weeks in Lübeck, and then boarded a vessel with many others. What is special about him is that he recorded his sea voyage in his poem *Travel Description of the Colonists and*

Russian Lifestyle of 1766-1767. "Roughly" translated, his poem tells about the waiting in Lübeck and the vessel boarding. It also tells that that everyone had food (at first) and was en route to Petersburg.

Their trip was made difficult by the wind and waves. The water became bad, rations gave out, and their pockets were empty from already purchasing provisions. The passengers had barely enough to survive by the time the trip ended. This trip lasted SIX weeks. Many settlers died during these voyages. A master baker Johannes Hühn, originally from Gelnhausen, testified in 1766 that he and the married couple Dolck and their two daughters were transported to Russia from Lübeck by a vessel belonging to Jakob Bauer. On the second day of the voyage, the daughters whom he had come to know very well, died of a sickness that had broken out. The dead were usually let go into the sea in front of the other passengers.[8]

Even on the voyages that went as planned, the colonists still suffered terribly. The ships were too small and the people were packed in as tightly as possible.

One colonist wrote of his ship voyage: "Since the majority of us had never been upon a ship, it was hard for the people to stand up because of the natural swaying of the boat. They tumbled against each other; fear and trembling mastered every mind; one cried, another swore, the majority prayed, yet in such a varied mixture that out of it all arose a strange woeful cry. Of the Catholics among us, some told there beads, one called on this saint, another on that; the Protestants uttered pious ejaculations from the Kubach, Schmolken and other prayer books. Finally, a Catholic struck up a litany and a Lutheran the song, "beu deine Wege." And now almost the whole crowd formed two choruses of which the first sang one song, the second the other."[9]

Arrival in Kronstadt

Most of my Volga Forefathers first stepped into Russia at the port at Kronstatdt which is part of the St. Petersburg's fortifications. From there, they were moved to a village a short distance west called Oranienbaum (now called Lomonosov). Here they were given temporary housing. Each family was required to complete paperwork by the Russian Emigration. While there, the colonists were able to obtain new clothing by using a ticket issued by their sheriff or foreman. They usually stayed around fourteen days in Oranienbaum, but their stay there could be indefinite.

One of the mandatory requirements for continuing on to the Volga was that they had to swear the oath of loyalty to the Russian Crown as set down in the 1763 Manifesto. Paragraph 5 of that document stated: *"On arrival, every foreigner intending to settle and registering themselves in the chancery set up for that purpose or in any other border town in Russia must confess his true intentions and swear an oath of loyalty according to the applicable religious ritual."*

The colonists swore this oath according to their religious affiliation in Oranienbaum. They assembled in the castle chapel with the oath being read out to them by Pastor Johann Christian König. The words were repeated by all present swearing the oath. At this point, everyone must have realized they had really become Russian subjects and return to Germany would be impossible.

Many, to keep their consciences clear and not be in breach of any future sworn oath should they return to their old countries, as Christian Gottlieb Züge wrote, *"merely moved their lips, without saying anything."*

Each colonist was also required to sign a contract that regulated all the goods and services due from the Russian side, and all rights <u>and duties</u> of each colonist. The contract was a formal agreement between the director, Baron Caneau de Beauregard, as the delegate of Catherine II for settlement of the colonies, and each colonist. Otto Friedrich von Monjou (a second director), also occasionally appears as signatory in place of Beauregard as does the authorized director Johann Friedrich Wilhelm von Nolting zu Schloss Fauerbach near Friedberg in the Wetterau.

The agreement detailed that the colonists were already in debt to the Russian government before they ever arrived. This debt grew with each cash advance during the transportation as follows: The colonist will receive for the journey from ... to St. Petersburg via Lübeck the sum of 15 Kreutzer per day, his wife 10, his children of marriageable age 10, and his minor children 6 Kreutzer per day. This money and the payments the colonists, their heirs and/or successors may receive after arrival (an "advance" of money or things) in Catherine The Greats' domain is to be repaid after 10 years in three installments over three years. No interest is payable. The crown will also pay transport costs from St. Petersburg to the place of settlement. In the event of departure from Russia within the next decade, only transport costs and the travel expenses subsidy to St. Petersburg is repayable. The colonist must then also pay a fifth of all his assets acquired in the first five years after arrival to the crown. If he leaves after only six to 10 years, then only a tenth is payable. Each colonist will receive money on arrival for purchases (animals, implements, home, barn, and seed). This is also repayable. Relief from all monetary taxation and obligatory rendering of good and/or services to the Russian crown for the next 30 years is granted.

Other areas covered by the contract were: Inheritance law was defined. Duty free import of goods to a value of 300 rubles was permitted on entry into Russia. The obligations of the Russian crown to each settler were also explained, as was freedom of religion and construction of properly built state schools for every religion. Medical services were guaranteed. Travel out of the country was permitted subject to conditions. Colonists received land (fields, pastures, woods and the like of best arable quality suited to maintain the entire family) on a hereditary leasehold. Colonists agreed to be loyal subjects of to adhere to Russian laws and customs, including those applying to the colonies. Annual payment of a tithe to their mayors and that mayors' right of first refusal at a price no higher than that demanded of third parties was promised.

More rules: Allocation of settlement areas on the Volga was to be in circular areas with a diameter of 60 to 70 versts (1 verst = 1.067 km) in each of which 100 families were to be settled. The number of colonies to be founded was 52 on the mountain side and 52 on the pasture side of the river. The settlers were to be allocated by Religion. Each family was to be given 30 *desjatines* of land on a hereditary leasehold. The land could not be split, sold or mortgaged and remained municipal property. Use of the land assigned was to be 15 *desjatines* for agriculture, 5 as pasture, 5 for dwelling and garden, plus 5 *desjatines* of woodland per family.

Inheritance - Primogeniture applied where only one son, the oldest, became sole heir. If he was unfit, the father could assign it to another son or relative. The aim of this provision was *"to ensure that every father knowing this law would make every effort to teach all his children a trade from infancy."*

Municipal self-government - Each colonist had to swear on arrival that he would adhere to the laws of the area. This legal code allowed the colonists to establish themselves as a separate class with considerable privileges and freedoms (of movement, import, export, transition to another class – citizen, military, clergy, and aristocracy). The Russians called them *wolnyje ljudi*, free people. The provisions of the Colonial Law and its supplements lasted for a century, but were revoked by the Russian Government in 1871.

After swearing the oath and contract signing, the families were then packed onto small ships for transport to St. Petersburg. They were not given housing, but were required to stay on the docked ships for as long as three weeks while at St. Petersburg.[10] While there, they were given detailed descriptions of their settlement areas, all supposedly unpopulated. The officials also registered all the assets each settler had with him.[11] All requirements had to be signed and completed, or they would stay indefinitely and live on the ship in deteriorating and unhealthy conditions.[12]

The Journey to Saratov

Each emigrant group was assigned to a Russian military leader and guards. They were tasked with leading and protecting the colonists on their trek to the Volga areas. Different routes were used. The entirely overland route went via Peterhof, Novgorod, Tver, Moscow, Riasan and Pensa to Pokrovsk (now called Engels) on the Volga, opposite Saratov. The water route proved better for larger groups. It led from St. Petersburg by ship and moved up the Neva River and Schluesselburg Canal to Lake Ladoga, up the Volkhov River to Novgorod. Any people sick remained at Novgorod to recover during the winter. If you were well, the trip continued via the Msta River to Vychni Volotchok.

Overland, the route went via Torshok, Tverza, Tver and then on the Volga to Yaroslavl, Kostroma and Nishni Novgorod, ending in Saratov. The colonists traveling by water were confronted with the same treatment as on the voyage from Lübeck. Again, captains tried to lengthen the voyage to force them to spend all their allowances on overpriced provisions. Eventually, they left the ships and the river and began following the land trail to the most northern navigable point of the Volga River at Torshok.[13] Women and children were jammed with the baggage on wagons. Men walked.

The trip continued via the Msta River to Vychni Volotchok. Their goal was to reach Torshok before it became winter and cold. Some did, but some did not make it until after the October snow. Many died of exposure and illness, and were buried on the way. The goal was to go as far as possible and they did not stop until the full winter had set in. Some were housed in Belosersk, Kyrilov, or Petrovsk. Those that reached Torshok safely usually stayed there over winter and lived with Russian peasants of near-by villages.[14]

While they were grateful to their hosts (who were paid by the Government to house them), the Germans were amazed that their Russian hosts kept their cattle, chickens, sheep, and pigs under the same roof with them.[15] When the Volga thawed in the Spring, the colonists again started on their way by ship down the river towards Saratov. Some continued on land to Kassimov to sail down the Oak River to the Volga.[16] Frequent river damage to the ships delayed and made travel even slower. Many died and were buried on Volga riverbanks. All wanted the journey to be over, and the forests along the Volga was rumored to have robbers and bandits.[17] They finally reached Saratov, which was the closest city to the settlement areas.

The overland route went via Peterhof, Novgorod, Tver, Moscow, Riasan and Pensa to Pokrovsk or "Kosakenstadt" or Cossacktown (now called Engels) on the Volga, opposite Saratov. The German name for Pokrovsk was "Kosakenstadt" or Cossacktown because most of the town people were Cossacks.[18] On their arrival in Saratov, the Voevodenkanzlei (Government office) issued to them 25 to 150 Rubles, depending on how many farm animals and tools they were given. They then continued to their final destinations. Grouped by destination village, those arriving in Saratov and going to the left side (Wiesenseite), moved by boat to Pokrovsk to join wagons headed south for those villages. If they arrived via Pokrovsk, then they would climb on the wagons going south.

Emigration Itinerary

1) Land & River Route from St Petersburg overland East to Volga River, follow Volga East to Samara, & the South to Saratov and Volga Colonies

OR

2) Land Route from St Petersburg overland Southeast to Moscow & Pensa, then South to Saratov and the Volga Colonies

Emigration Path - St. Petersburg to Saratov [19]

The distance covered was around two thousand miles. Many families took more than a year to complete it. After all that, you would think they deserved a break… Life had other plans.

The Settlements

Settlement areas were mainly on the steppes near the Volga that had strategic military value to Russia. These areas were named as the governorships of Samara and Saratov. Between 1765 and 1770, 104 colonies were founded. The first, founded by Protestant settlers in 1764, was named Catherinenstadt (Baronsk in Russian, later Marxstadt). By

1772, this colony had a population of 283. Glaka, founded in 1772 on the mountainside of the Volga, had 459. Catholic colony Mariental, founded in 1776, had 400 inhabitants. Protestant Warenburg, founded in 1767, had 592 in 1772.[20]

Bergseite & Wiesenseite Map [21]

The Volga colony area is about 450 miles southeast of Moscow, on either side of the Volga River. Saratov was the only large Russian city in the area. The land on either side of the Volga River varies greatly with the Bergseite (meaning hillside) or west side of the river having banks that rose steeply to a wooded hills traversed and deep gorges covered with tall grass and bushes.

The settlements by the German colonists began about thirty miles south of Saratov and ended north of Kamyshin. Only ten of the villages were near the Volga River, with all the others some distance west along smaller rivers whose waters flowed westward into the Don. Of those 104 original mother colonies, forty-five were on the Westside (Bergseite). This area corresponded to the Saratov province. Occasionally our ancestors would list the name of the province, either Saratov or Samara on their paperwork as their home instead of the name of their village.

On the Wiesenseite (meaning meadow side), or east side of the river, lay a low-level grassy plain gently sloping towards the river with small slow creeks. One area of settlement began about twenty miles upstream from Saratov and continued northeastward up the Volga and eastward along both the Great and the Little Karman Rivers. My ancestors' villages were farther south about fifty miles downstream. Sixty-six mother colonies were started on the Wiesenseite.[22]

Contemplating the Volga [23]

Chapter 2
The Bad
Shock & Disappointment

No one got any breaks. After the long and difficult journey, the colonists who survived were challenged with many difficulties. They were shocked when they found the actual condition of land they had traveled so far to reach.

One of the Colonists, Christian Gottlieb Züge, wrote of the first impressions of their new land. *"Our leader cried stop! It surprised us greatly as it was too early to camp for the night. This surprise soon changed to amazement and shock when we were told that this was our final destination. We exchanged looks of amazement at finding ourselves in a wilderness of meter-high grass with nothing else visible all around except for a small wood. None made any effort to descend from horse or wagon and as soon as we had recovered from our shock to some extent every face showed a desire to turn back. So this is the paradise promised by the Russian recruiters in Lübeck, one of my fellow sufferers exclaimed with a sad face. Admittedly, it had been stupid of us to expect an uninhabited Garden of Eden. The disappointment of finding a steppe that fulfilled none of our needs was almost unbearable. We saw no signs in the area of any attempt to welcome us in any way either then or later, although as winter was coming it seemed urgently necessary to get to work."*

Züge continued in his writings that the materials that the Government had promised for house construction were not available. All that had been done was to roughly lay out spaces for the houses. The Government told them that there were no houses built because there was no lumber available locally. All the lumber had been ordered, but it had to be floated down the Volga River from as far away as Viatka (over 300 miles North). Once it floated as close as possible by river, the lumber still had to be dragged by horses to the village sites.[24] The sheer numbers of colonists and required housing evidently overwhelmed the Russians.

Luckily, native Russians from surrounding villages must have felt sorry for the strange new people. They warned the German colonists that without adequate housing they would not survive the rapidly approaching winter.

The Russians offered to teach them how to build partially underground huts patterned after those of the some of the wild tribes living nearby.[25] These shelters, called "semlinken or semlyanka" were big enough for three or four families to live together in. With little or no ventilation and the crowded conditions, it was only the minimum for survival during the harsh Russian winters.[26]

Christian Gottlieb Züge described the people from Lübeck who were his companions on their trek to the settlement area on the Volga. His view was not very complimentary. I should mention that Züge felt that since he was a "member of an honorable trade" that he could look down on his fellow travelers (farmers and peasants) with arrogance.

His comments: "Rejects who sought unknown parts since their homelands had spat them out or threatened to do so. Amoral folk able to find comfort in any situation as long as they could give their lust unbridled rein formed a second class equally unpleasant. The third class, smallest of all, consisted of unfortunates or persecuted people. The fourth and most numerous was made up of adventurers and the easily influenced, willing to do anything if it were only sold them well enough, or inexperienced types seduced by the recruiters and who really believed mountains of gold existed as promised." [27]

History records that Christian Gottlieb Züge was never satisfied. He escaped the Volga Colonies and returned to Germany in 1774.

While Christian Gottlieb Züge may have been one of those people never satisfied, others shared his views. One new settler remarked, *"We looked at each other with frightened expressions. We were in a wilderness without even a tree. Nothing was to be seen except the endless dry grass of the steppes."* [28]

The Death Rate

If their disappointment was not bad enough, the colonists felt even worse because they were homesick for Germany, for relatives they had left, and for the family members that died on the way. [29]

The records do not tell us how many died during the trips from Germany to the Volga Colonies, but they do tell us that out of the 7,501 people listed on the 1766-1767 Transport Lists, an unbelievable 1,264 or 16.9% died between Oranienbaum to Saratov. The records also tell us that approximately 6,200 (82.5%) out of the 7,501 actually made it to Saratov. The percentage that died or became lost or missing was a total of 17.5%. [30] Another record gives a lower death rate of 12.5% (3,293) for the total 26,676 colonists that traveled from Oranienbaum to Saratov. [31] Even the lower number of 3,293 dead is unsettling.

The Wild Weather

The climate was in no way like anything the recruiters promised. It was much more extreme than what was normal in

Germany. The soil was salty and sandy, and good water was hard to find. Most of the colonists had fallen for the promise of good air and fertile soil in the settlement areas, like that on the upper Rhine back in Germany.

They thought they were moving to a country something like Italy or Germany. On the Volga, however, they found the climate to be one of wide extremes. It was nothing like what they were used to, or anything like Italy or Germany.

Since most rain fell between October and April, their field plowing and sowing had to be deep and at the right time to guarantee the seed did not dry out. Strong winds in March and April dried the ground out. They had to allow for late frosts that could kill the harvest. Snowstorms were common in winter causing drifts that covered the field with snow. In between the snows, there would be mild weather that melted the snow, but then the next frost turned the fields into sheets of ice. Hail showers could also ruin the crops.

The Sickness

The colonists were plagued with a sickness that killed many, and sometimes even wiped out entire families.[32] Some thought it was just homesickness or despair for their new life, but the fever caused many of all ages and sex to die.[33]

There was also a frequent typhus-like sickness that usually, but not always, came around in the Spring. Sometimes it also visited in the Fall. Records tell that in one village it appeared only two months after the colonists' arrival. During the time from September thru January, 15% of the village died from it. Entire families were killed by this sickness.[34]

It is thought that there were three main causes for this recurring sickness. The first was the poor housing available for many of them. Those that had to build the dug-out homes (semlinken or semlyanka) to survive the cold, often built in the middle of the forests or close to the riverbanks.

Both locations were unhealthy. The forest air was damp and moldy. The air was made even worse inside the dug-outs with the crowded conditions and minimal ventilation. Those that built near the river usually did so near the riverbends or in low places where they would be sheltered from the harsh winter winds and snows. Their plan worked and they were protected from "Old Man Winter."

Unfortunately, when the snow thawed and melted in the Spring, the rivers rose and flooded their huts. This left them with absolutely nothing and nowhere to live in a village already struggling to survive.[35]

The second cause was the climate. The unexpected temperature changes in the Spring and Fall, along with the poor housing, caused the colonists to be cold more often with little resistance to sickness. Those that survived eventually did acclimatize to the weather.

The third cause was the brackish water that some of the Colonies that were not near free running rivers used for their drinking water supply.

Food Shortages

Another cause of the sickness could have been the shortage of food those first few years.

The land is different on each side of the Volga, and it took time for the farmers to develop productive methods for growing food. One common characteristic of many Russian rivers is that the eastern bank is flat and the other bank is steep.

Bergseite
*(steep banks of the Volga with
forested hills and deep gorges)*

Medveditsa
River

Rosenheim

• Katharinenstadt
Malo Karaman
River

Saratov•

Bolshoi
Karaman
River

•Engels

• Stahl
Karamysh   • Kukkus   Nachoi River
Norka.   River   •Lauwe
Walter•   Anton•   •Jost
Kutter   •   •Laub
Frank•   Donhof•   Balzer   Tarlyk River
Dietal•   . Dinkel
Rothammel•   •Grimm   • Straub
Schuck•   •Warenburg   Krasnyy-Kut
Medveditsa
River   Vollmer•   Seelmann
Kamenka Volga River
Pfeifer•
Kohler•   Kraft
•Holstein
Marienfeld •   Dobrinka   Jersulan River

Ilawla River

Kamyshin•

Wiesenseite
*(low grassy plain sloping
gently towards the Volga)*

Bergseite & Wiesenseite Map [36]

They called the left bank of the Volga in the settlement area
the "pasture side" and the right bank the "mountain side." The
pasture side had swamp areas on the riverbanks. The fields in
this flood area had thick plant growth and were used by the
Volga Germans for hay and cow pastures.

The bordering steppe was especially suited to wheat after having been made fit for farming. This was never before used land and it took many months to till the land. The other bank was steep with many streams.

Settlers on the flatter side had ample land to expand available, but those on the opposite bank could not expand because native Russian farmers lived on the bordering lands.

Since the new Colonists did not have experience with this type of soil or climate, it took years before they could survive on their farm harvest and production.

Actually, it took a decade before they had enough experience to be masters of the land as they had been in Germany. Until that time there was never enough food for all.

Along with the wild weather, there were hordes of mice and gophers to add to large crop losses. Soil quality on the mountainside and a pasture side with the river in the middle let them grow wheat, barley, watermelon, potatoes, flax and sunflowers. Woad, an herb grown for the blue dyestuff from the leaves, also grew there.

Even with all those hardships, they did eventually succeed as farmers eventually. By 1798 (a little over thirty years since the colonies were founded), most of the colonies had at least one flourmill, a public granary, and gardens. Some even had orchards and apiaries. Most had not introduced fertilizing. They were able to grow a variety of crops to include, rye, wheat, barley, oats, millet, peas, potatoes, and tobacco.

Artisans No- Farmers Yes

The German scientist (zoologist and botanist and Professor at the St. Petersburg Academy of Science) Peter Simon Pallas wrote comments on the economic development of the

Volga Colonies in his book *Journey Through the Various Provinces in Russia* (published in 1773). He also mentioned the various trades and crafts of the colonists. For many, the dream of performing their trades was not allowed. They were forced to be satisfied as farmers.

As noted before, while the Recruiters would promise that a prospective colonist would be able to perform his trade, in reality what was needed and what was allowed in the Volga Colonies was only farming.

Author Gottlieb Beratz probably described it best; *"Here stood a tailor; there wigmaker; neither of them had ever harnessed a horse, not to mention worked in the fields, but nevertheless they were given an old Kalmuck horse, and a few pieces of lumber with which to make a plow and a wagon, and were calmly told to get to work."*[37] When and if the farming was finished, than the trades and crafts would be allowed to be practiced.

There were some that felt that since they had never plowed land back in Germany, they were not going to farm in the Colonies.

The Office of the Guardianship Chancery for Foreigners or Kontor in Saratov had one answer for this, *"You have to become farmers now, there is no alternative."*[38] Failure to comply was felt to be disobedience or laziness. The Kontor would use the appropriate means to convince both the disobedient or lazy person to see the error of their ways.[39]

One of the methods used is explained in the following letter of October 4, 1768 from the Kontor: *"Order to the overseer of the colony Kopenka, Nicholas Vollmar: the colonist Johannes Husz, belonging to your colony, who was condemned this past summer, for his laziness and bad management of his farm, to work in the brick factory in the colony Rossoshi, which work is now finished, is being sent back to you in the custody of a Cossack, with the instruction that he be put to work by you and that you keep him incessantly and exactly under observation. You are to report to the Kontor that he has been brought to you."* [40]

Those that did not see the error of their ways after a term of forced labor in a "brick factory," could look forward to serving time in the penitentiary in Saratov.[41] Most wisely became farmers...

Volga Area Appropriate Sign [42]

Chapter 3
More Bad
Tsarina Catherine the Great

The events that led up to colonists movement started with the birth of Sofia Augusta Fredrieka into the royal line of Anhalt-Zerbst of Prussia in Stettin (now Szczecin, Poland) on May 2, 1729.[43] She was the eldest child of Prince Christian August, and her nickname was Fike. She is reputed as being an aggressive learner and a well-educated woman. With the help and approval of the Russian Empress Elizabeth, she became wife of the next heir to the Russian throne, Peter III.[44]

As she was originally of the Lutheran Faith, Sofia had to be baptized into the Russian Orthodox Church in 1774 and was given the Orthodox name Catherine Alexeyevna. She married the future heir to the Russian throne, Duke Peter of Holstein-Gottorp. In 1761, with the death of Empress Elizabeth, Peter III became the ruler of Russia.

As his wife, Catherine Alexeyevna (Sophia/Fike) was christened as Catherine II. Apparently, Peter III was not prepared to become the ruler. In 1762, he was overthrown and murdered by Catherine and her palace courtiers.[45] And so following an overnight change of power, the daughter of a noble Prussian family became Empress of Russia Catherine the Great.

Most researchers over the past two hundred years have reinforced the idea that Tsarina Catherine the Great was a kindly, benevolent ruler only looking out for the welfare of the German colonists. My research led me to a much darker view of the ruler. First, that sweet, benevolent ruler idea does not balance with what history tells us about her involvement with the overthrow and eventual murder of her husband, Peter III.

Second, her primary goal was to raise her Russia's cultural and political status. She had great plans for the future of Russia. Many never succeeded. Her power base was extremely fragile, and she had no actual legal right to the throne.

She needed the support of the Russian aristocracy who had looked the other way when she had her husband removed from the throne. Catherine had to have their approval and cooperation in order for anything to work.[46]

The Volga area that my ancestors settled was of strategic military importance to Russia. Over the centuries, Russia had tried many times with little success to stabilize and civilize the area. The settlement of the Volga Germans into the area by Tsarina Catherine the Great was a final solution to this age-old problem that no previous ruler had been able to fix.

This was not the first attempt of Catherine the Great to civilize the Volga area. She had first tried in1762 to induce (seduce) Russian peasants to move to and live in the area. The Russian peasants already knew of the harsh conditions and the constant danger of attack. No one took the bait, and the plan failed.

Ok, try and try again. Her second plan to civilize the Volga area involved issuing a royal invitation or manifesto welcoming people of all nationalities except Jews to come and live there. Again, no one took the bait, and the plan failed.

Third try… and she was unimagineably successful. Catherine the Great issued a second manifesto on June 22, 1763. She sweetened the offer by promising 1) that the colonists could settle in any area of Russia, 2) Russia would pay all travel expenses, 3) freedom of religion, 4) freedom from taxes for thirty years, 5) freedom from military service, and 6) their own self-government. [47] Whether she had any intention of living up to those promises is unknown. In any case, she and her Government reneged on some from the very start, and eventually broke all.

Promise 1:

Manifesto of the Empress Catherine II

Issued July 22, 1763

By the Grace of God!

We, Catherine the second, ……. of Our intention the following decree which We hereby solemnly establish and order to be carried out to the full.

*We permit all foreigners to come into Our Empire, in order **to settle in all the gouvernements, just as each one may desire**.*

*As soon as these foreigners arrive in Our residence and report at the Guardianship Chancellery or in a border-town, they shall be required to state their true decision whether their real desire is to be enrolled in the guild of merchants or artisans, and become citizens, and in what city; or if they wish to settle on free, productive land in colonies and rural areas, to take up agriculture or some other useful occupation. **Without delay, these people will be assigned to their destination, according to their own wishes and desires.** From the following register* it can be seen in which regions of Our Empire free and suitable lands are still available. However, besides those listed, there are many more regions and all kinds of land where We will **likewise permit people to settle, just as each one chooses for his best advantage.***

The offer that the colonists could settle in any area of Russia was taken back just as soon as the colonists set foot in Russia at St Petersburg. The emigrants had two choices, 1) go be farmers in the Volga area, or 2) they would be released and could return to Germany just as soon as they immediately paid the Russian Government back all the money it had spent on food, housing and transport to get them to St Petersburg. These were poor people, and the Russian Government knew that they had the colonists in a strangle hold. So much for promise 1. [48]

Promise 2:

Manifesto of the Empress Catherine II

Issued July 22, 1763

By the Grace of God!

We, Catherine the second, ……. of Our intention the following decree which We hereby solemnly establish and order to be carried out to the full.

*Since those foreigners who would like to settle in Russia will also include some who do not have sufficient means to pay the required travel costs, they can report to our ministers in foreign courts, who will not only **transport them to Russia at Our expense, but also provide them with travel money.***

Russia would pay all travel expenses was promise #2. In fact, what Russia meant was that they would provide the money for traveling "up front" and the emigrants would have to pay it back with interest over their lifetime and their descendants' lifetimes. Of course, this was not explained fully until they set foot in Russia. So much for promise #2.

Promise 3:

Manifesto of the Empress Catherine II

Issued July 22, 1763

By the Grace of God!

We, Catherine the second, ……. of Our intention the following decree which We hereby solemnly establish and order to be carried out to the full.

We grant to all foreigners coming into Our Empire the free and unrestricted practice of their religion according to the precepts and usage of their Church. *To those, however, who intend to settle not in cities but in colonies and villages on uninhabited lands we grant the freedom to build churches and belltowers, and to maintain the necessary number of priests and church servants, but not the construction of monasteries. On the other hand, everyone is hereby warned not to persuade or induce any of the Christian co-religionists living in Russia to accept or even assent to his faith or join his religious community, under pain of incurring the severest punishment of Our law. This prohibition does not apply to the various nationalities on the borders of Our Empire who are attached to the Mahometan faith. We permit and allow everyone to win them over and make them subject to the Christian religion in a decent way.*

Promise #3 was kept for about 100 years. Eventually around 1860 the Russian Government began to force the Russian Orthodox religion on everyone. At first, you did not have to become Russian Orthodox, but if you did not, you could not own any land or property. Eventually, their was no freedom of religion. So much for promise #3.

Promise 4:

Manifesto of the Empress Catherine II

Issued July 22, 1763

By the Grace of God!

We, Catherine the second, ……. of Our intention the following decree which We hereby solemnly establish and order to be carried out to the full.

None of the foreigners who have come to settle in Russia shall be required to pay the slightest taxes to Our treasury, *nor be forced to render regular or extraordinary services, nor to billet troops. Indeed, everybody shall be exempt from all taxes and tribute in the following manner: those who have been settled as colonists with their families in hitherto uninhabited regions **will enjoy 30 years of exemption**; those who have established themselves, at their own expense, in cities as merchants and tradesmen in Our Residence St. Petersburg or in the neighboring cities of Livland, Esthonia, Ingermanland, Carelia and Finland, as well as in the Residential city of Moscow, shall enjoy 5 years of tax-exemption. Moreover, each one who comes to Russia, not just for a short while but to establish permanent domicile, shall be granted free living quarters for half a year.*

Freedom from taxes for thirty years was #4. The colonists could not keep up with the principal and interest payments on the "front money", much less pay taxes. Empty promise.

Promise 5:

Manifesto of the Empress Catherine II

Issued July 22, 1763

By the Grace of God!

We, Catherine the second, ……. of Our intention the following decree which We hereby solemnly establish and order to be carried out to the full.

The foreigners who have settled in Russia **shall not be drafted against their will into the military or the civil service during their entire stay here.** *Only after the lapse of the years of tax-exemption can they be required to provide labor service for the country. Whoever wishes to enter military service will receive, besides his regular pay, a gratuity of 30 rubles at the time he enrolls in the regiment.*

Promise #5 was freedom from military service. Again, this did last about 100 years before it was discarded.

Promise 6:

Manifesto of the Empress Catherine II

Issued July 22, 1763

By the Grace of God!

We, Catherine the second, ……. of Our intention the following decree which We hereby solemnly establish and order to be carried out to the full.

We leave to the discretion of the established colonies and village the internal constitution and jurisdiction, **in such a way that the persons placed in authority by Us will not interefere with the internal affairs and institutions. In other respects the colonists will be liable to Our civil laws.** *However, in the event that the people would wish to have a special guardian or even an officer with a detachment of disciplined soldiers for the sake of security and defense, this wish would also be granted.*

The last promise was self-government. This never existed. From the very start the villages of the Volga were either under the thumb of the Recruiter Agents or of the Russian Government Agents. There was no way the Russian Government was going to allow a bunch of Germans freedom to do what they wanted. The Government did allow them more freedom than they allowed to their own Russian peasants.... Which was no freedom at all!

As I read though the Manifesto, I am struck by the number of conflicting passages in it. For example, in regards to taxes, the Manifesto states: *"None of the foreigners who have come to settle in Russia shall be required to pay the slightest taxes to Our treasury."* Three sentences later it also states:" *will enjoy 30 years of exemption."*

In regards to self-government, it states:" *in such a way that the persons placed in authority by Us will not interefere with the internal affairs and institutions."* The very next sentence is conflicting and vague in stating:" *In other respects the colonists will be liable to Our civil laws.*"

I am aware that language has changed over the years and the translation may not be perfect, but this was an extremely difficult contract to understand. Whether it was designed that way so the Russian Government could change their definition of its' meaning at will (which they did), or whether it was just poorly written is not known.

Remember that the German colonists were mostly poor people that had little if any school education. It is doubtful if any of them could read what they were agreeing to..... They would just have to take the word of the Recruiter agents when they signed up, or the Russian agents along the way. This might be the main reason so many of them were "fooled" into participating in this wild scheme of Catherine the Great.

So why did they leave Germany? Karl Stumpp wrote in his book Emigration from Germany to Russia from 1763 to 1862:

"There was never a single reason for emigration. Several reasons always came together with one dominating in one area and another elsewhere.[49] You have to look at all the reasons: WAR, TAXATION, ECONOMIC STABILITY, POPULATION GROWTH & INHERITANCE, RELIGION, and the GRASS IS ALWAYS GREENER.

War

War happened in my Ancestor's time and War still exists today for the same basic reasons. One group has something another group wants (political or power), or one group believes in something another group "knows" is wrong (religion).

The areas of Germany from which most of the emigrants came suffered under repeated military conflict from the beginning of the Thirty Years War all the way to the early 19th century. People migrating (or fleeing) from such areas became the norm, and at this time Germany was just recovering from the Seven-Years War.

The Seven Years' War (1754 and 1756–1763) had Great Britain, Prussia, and Hannover on one side and France, Austria, Russia, Sweden, and Saxony on the opposing side. Spain and Portugal were later drawn into the conflict.[50] The conflict existed all around the world, but for this book the most important area of battle is in western Germany north of the Main River. Areas of Saxony, Hannover, Brunswick, Hesse-Kassel, and Wurttemberg were constantly battled over[51] with Hesse-Kassel frequently involved.

The cities of Kassel and Marburg were captured and regained five times in the fighting between the French and the Northern Hessian troops. The fighting was not just in those cities, but carried over to hundreds of miles in every direction.[52] By 1763, treaties had been signed again, and the land was peaceful. Remember this date, as it appears to be very important in my ancestors' decisions.

From the countless and almost continuous military conflicts came such negative results as looting, forced military service, forced requisitioning of supplies by both armies, and increased taxation by whoever won.

Someone had to pay for the War, and it was always the peasants. Someone had to fill the soldier's ranks, and so forced conscription to military service was harshly carried out. Today we call it the "Draft", and the affects were the same today or back then. During Viet Nam, our youth fled to Canada; in 1765, they fled to Russia (among other places).

Along with the high war taxation, a post-war economic depression with an enormous increase in the cost of living occurred. Sounds like modern times. Add the changing climate that caused many complete losses of harvests. This made food scarce and forced prices up with the lowest classes hit the hardest. Grain price increases led to more frequent famines from 1760 on.

Taxation

Taxation is a necessity of Government. The Government has no money of its' own. The people have it all. Taxation and War go hand in hand. As the cost of War increased, taxes would also increase to the point that eventually the tax burdens of a farm owed to the state and to the landowner exceeded farm income. The profit from sales of agricultural produce and animal farming were the major sources of rural income.

To pay the increasing tax burden, some of the producing animals had to be sacrificed and sold off. Less producing animals meant less profit and even more unpaid tax burden. The total farming income kept decreasing. Taxes never decreased, as the population also had to foot the bill for their ruler lord's expensive household budget in addition to the war and occupation costs.

The smaller the farm, the higher the proportionate load. Small farms were the norm and they failed first. The peasant farmers were faced with increasing debt and loss of their farms to the foreclosure auction.

These foreclosure sales eventually happened so often that the Hessian government adopted preventative measures such as the granting interest-free loans and repayment on installment plans to keep farmers from emigrating.

Economic Stability

The loss of harvests due to war and weather forced food kept the lowest classes barely existing. They lived to eat to live. Famines happened repeatedly. Escalating food prices caused demand for goods and services of all kinds to drop. This reduced income in artisans' trades. Today we call that an economic recession or depression.

As for stability, try to imagine having the country you are a citizen of change every few months or years with different rules, customs, and laws. One day you were a citizen of Hesse, the next day of France, and the next day of Prussia. All this traveling from area to another with out ever moving.

Population Growth & Inheritance

Continuous growth in population in Germany through the 18th century brought the total to around 22 million. All these people led to a shortage of land where no one could own his own farm. The number of people living solely from their own land dropped. At the same time, the rural poor and landless became more numerous. A second income was essential to many for survival.

What land that was available was either infertile or owned by a large landowner that dictated the obligations and servitude of the serfs working his lands. These obligations and servitude often meant poverty-line existence for the workers. Some escaped to the larger villages and urban areas to try to learn a rural trade, but these were also tied to some type of obligations or servitude and offered only limited opportunities of earning a livelihood.

The customary Inheritance laws also provided another reason to leave. One law set down that only one heir could inherit the entire farm. All other heirs were to be compensated. Even so, they had to work as farm laborers or milkmaids to live, and suffered a drop in class status and living standards to the level of the landless peasantry. They might be able to get their own farm by purchase, marriage or emigration elsewhere (unless domestic expansion was limited by soil quality). They might be forced to find employment in urban trade or industry. This was "the law of entail" that was used in northern Germany.

Completely opposite, another region's customary inheritance law resulted in each child receiving an equal portion of the land inherited by all. Seems a lot fairer, but there was huge negative side. The splitting up of the land for each generation led to increasingly smaller farms that eventually resulted in small individual farms unable to support any family.

This happened at the end of the 18th century on a large scale. About two-thirds of the rural population could no longer survive on the land available to them. Opportunities to earn money in other ways to help them survive were also very limited. The prospect was a life of permanent poverty. One way out for many was emigration to Russia.

Religion

One of the causes of War is Religion, i.e. the Crusades, the Thirty Year War, and the Seven Year War. Just as it is today, membership in a particular denomination or church or religion was often accompanied by sanctions and persecution or death, as well as financial hardship. This all too frequent persecution motivated many to migrate to include Lutherans, Reformed Faith, Catholics, and Mennonites (among others).

Grass is Always Greener

There are always people around that have struggled with the "greener grass syndrome." They feel that the grass is always greener on the other side of the fence. Their only answer to their unhappiness with life is to move on because it just has to be better over there than it is here. Those that migrated to the Russia for this reason were in for big disappointments.

For whatever reasons, Tsarina Catherine the Greats' third try at seducing the colonists was an overwhelming success for Russia. There was one additional reason that may have helped sway the German colonist to listen to Catherine the Great.

The reason was that she was born a German, and the colonists believed she was one of their countrymen. She would not lie to her own people so they believed in her. Unfortunately, while the plan was a winner for Russia, it was not a success for those colonists that believed her.

Great or Not So Great

Tsarina Catherine the Great was well aware of the dangers and risks that the uncivilized and native people of the area posed to the German settlers. However, her first responsibility was to Mother Russia and if some of her former countrymen died at the hands of the robbers and uncivilized, so be it.

In every war, there were bound to be sacrifices and there were plenty of fools still in Germany ready to come to Mother Russia. The Tsarina used her former countrymen (and my ancestors) as a human barrier to keep out the unwanted and uncivilized to extend her power.

Painting of Catherine the Great [53]

Was she a Kind, Benevolent Ruler

or

Painting of Catherine the Great [54]

A Scheming, Manipulative Monarch?

Four additional questions come to mind when I contemplate the first question above.....

1) If you had a goal and because of the way you accomplished that goal almost FOUR THOUSAND innocent men, women, and children died unknowingly trying to help you fulfill that goal, What do they call you?

2) If you sent Thousands of innocent men, women, and children into known dangers and probable death without any warning, What do they call you?

3) If you lied, or paid others to lie and promise things that were not true to seduce or fool even more innocent men and women to risk their lives and the lives of their children to help you succeed, What do they call you?

4) If you really are guilty of the first three and risked nothing yourself while innocent men, women, and children risked all, What should they call you?

I suppose it is not fair to use hindsight to evaluate the actions of or life of Catherine the Great. Nor is it fair to judge her using today's standards. Maybe the only way to evaluate her actions fairly is to consider this one last question.

What if my German ancestors and all the other the Germans who were seduced by her promises and moved to the Volga had never heard of her or her proposals? What if they had never moved and remained living their lives in Germany? Would they, their families, and their descendants been better off?

After having lived almost three years in Germany, I honestly believe that they would have been better off never knowing of Catherine the Great or her proposal, and that they and their descendants would have had better lives by remaining in Germany.

The Palace of Catherine the Great [55]

Chapter 4
Still More Bad
Robber Bands

Prior to the settlement of the Volga area by the Colonists, this area of Russia was infested with the "less fortunate" such as deserters, vagabonds, and robbers who had found hiding places in and along the gorges of the Medveditza, Karamysh and Ilovlya (or Ilavla) rivers.

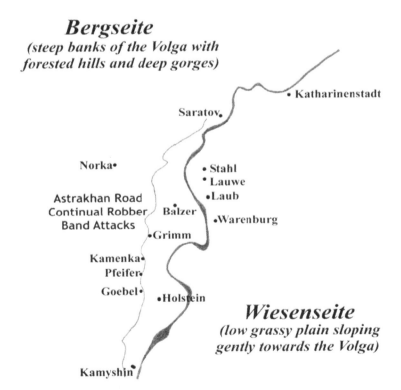

Bergseite
(steep banks of the Volga with forested hills and deep gorges)

• Katharinenstadt

Saratov•

Norka•

• Stahl
• Lauwe
•Laub

Astrakhan Road
Continual Robber   Balzer
Band Attacks
•Grimm

•Warenburg

Kamenka•
Pfeifer•

Goebel•   •Holstein

Wiesenseite
(low grassy plain sloping gently towards the Volga)

Kamyshin•

Astrakhan Road along the Volga River [56]

These "less fortunate" were especially prevalent in the exact region of the later German settlements on the Bergseite side of the Volga. Before the Germans arrived, the area was extremely poor and there was not much for any criminal to prey on. However, after the founding of the German Volga Colonies, there was the mass influx of people and goods. This was a rich booty for those willing to steal and murder.

Since the territory was already very familiar to the Robbers (and not to the new colonists), there was little risk of capture. Almost immediately, the robber economy became very profitable. Even more robber bands formed because of the easy availability to "acquire" goods. The robbers were even more frequent on the Bergseite because the great Astrakhan highway ran through the colonies there, and the hilly terrain provided good hiding features.

Local Peoples and Indigenous Nomads

On top of the Robber problem, conflicts with the local people and indigenous nomads often caused loss of property and deaths. One of the things we seem to forget is that this area of the Russia had been inhabited by many different groups long before Catherine the Great offered their land to the German colonists. These groups had been fighting over control of this area for thousands of years, and had been fighting the influence of Moscow for hundreds of years. Their response to a mass of German colonists moving on to their lands at the decree of a woman ruler in Moscow could not have been good. To them, these Germans were outsiders who deserved no quarter and needed to be subjugated.... Just as they had subjugated any weaker tribes or people over the past thousand years. For these reasons, the German colonists traveling the roads were prime targets. Eventually, the colonists learned that for their own safety they should always be armed and in groups of five or ten when they left their villages.

Kirghiz and Kazakh

The Kirghiz belonged to the westernmost branch or inner horde of the ethnic group called the Kazakhs.[57] They were essentially nomads concerned with the breeding of small but hardy horses, a fat-tailed type of sheep, oxen used both for riding and as pack animals, some goats, and camels of both species.

Physically they were a middle-sized, square-built race, stout, with long black hair, minimal beard, with small, black and oblique eyes, broad Mongoloid features, high cheekbones, broad, flat nose, small mouth, very small hands and feet, and brown or swarthy complexion. Their farming was limited to the cultivation of wheat, barley and millet, The term Kirghiz is never used by the steppe nomads, who always call themselves simply Kazakhs, which was commonly interpreted as riders.[58]

The tribes of the Kirghiz and Kazakh attacked often. The first attack of the Kirghiz occurred in August 1771. They struck two colonies that were the farthest out. Most men were out working in the fields when a band of 50 tribesmen attacked the villages. Because only a few people were at home, the Kirghiz could steal without any opposition.Unfortunately, they were not content with just taking away the livestock and other property, but also took the colonists as prisoners. They could sell them into slavery in Bukhara and Khiva.

The two colonies were abandoned as a result of this Kirghiz attack. Those who escaped capture moved to neighboring settlements.

Drawing of Nomadic Tribesman attacking German Colonists [59]

In 1772, the colony of Caesarfeld founded in 1774 was attacked by Kazakh or Kirghiz tribesman and destroyed. The Catholic village of Chaisol was destroyed in 1774. The second attack on the Karaman in the colony of Mariental took place in August 1774. All livestock and people and property was stolen and carried off across the Ural River into the Russian steppe. The total number of captives taken away from Mariental was about 300, of which very few ever came back. After the attack, six wagons were loaded with bodies from the murder site and buried in two large graves in the cemetery of Mariental. Missing bodies were later found on the steppe or in the forest shot with Kirghiz arrows. Those captives that survived (mostly women and children) were eventually sold by the Kirghiz into the harems of wealthy Mohammedans in areas under the control of Turkey.[60]

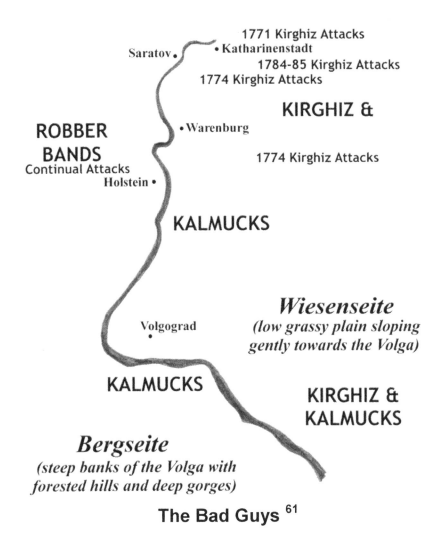

1771 Kirghiz Attacks

Saratov•

• Katharinenstadt

1784-85 Kirghiz Attacks

1774 Kirghiz Attacks

KIRGHIZ &

ROBBER

BANDS

Continual Attacks

• Warenburg

1774 Kirghiz Attacks

Holstein •

KALMUCKS

Wiesenseite

(low grassy plain sloping

gently towards the Volga)

Volgograd
•

KALMUCKS

KIRGHIZ &

KALMUCKS

Bergseite

(steep banks of the Volga with

forested hills and deep gorges)

The Bad Guys [61]

On October 24, 1774, the Kazakh or Kirghiz attacked the colonies Seelmann, Leitsinger, Keller, and Holzel, and carried away 317 persons. These people were sold into slavery in minor Bukhara. In 1776, the colony of Mariental was attacked and its inhabitants captured. One hundred fifty men from the neighboring Protestant village Catherinenstadt rushed to their aid under the leadership of Pastor Wernborner. They were also captured. Suposedly, the sound of the church bell that

43

called the believers to public worship led the Kazakh tribesmen to the village location. The story of the subsequent attack exists still in *"Schön Ammi von Mariental und der Kirgisen-Michel, a Picture of the Volga Steppe from the 18th Century"*. One record tells that the pastor (probably Pastor Wernborner) had his tongue cut out, and that hundreds of people were beheaded, speared, trampled by horses, or drowned in nearby streams.[62]

Kazakh-Kirghiz tribesman kidnapped 1,573 settlers from colonies in 1774. Only half were successfully ransomed with the rest killed or enslaved. Their families might receive messages from the kidnapped asking for ransom 20 years later. Over the next 25 years some of the captured did return either by escape or ransom.

To stop this raiding, the colonies on the Wiesenseite sent armed patrols to the Ural steppe. They also developed signal fires to give warning of impending attack. They formulated defense strategies, including some government help, which decreased the incursion raids of the Kazakh-Kirghiz.

The last attack on the colonies by the Kazakh-Kirghiz was on August 16, 1785 on the villages of Chasselois and Louis. A woman, child, and four elderly colonists were killed, and 130 colonists were taken prisoner during the attack. Government forces quickly caught the attackers as they were moving their prisoners. In the resulting battle, 70 Kazakh-Kirghiz were killed and all the colonists were freed.[63]

Kalmucks & Gypsies

The Kalmucks (Kalmyks)) were a different story. The Kalmucks were a semi nomadic branch of the Oirat Mongols.

They migrated from Chinese Turkistan to the steppe west of the Volga's mouth in the mid-17th cent. They became independent allies of the Russians and were tasked with guarding the eastern frontier of the Russian Empire by Tsar Peter I. Under Catherine II, however, the Kalmyks became dependent servants of Russia.

Kalmuck Territory [64]

In 1771, without asking Catherine the Great, about 300,000 Kalmyks east of the Volga River set out to return to China. They were annihilated in route by attacks of Russians, Kazakhs, and Kyrgyz that Catherine had ordered.[65]

The Kalmyks west of the Volga River remained in the Volga River area of Russia. They roamed the border area of the settlements, but they never attacked or plundered any colony. They did carry out petty thievery and stole horses when they had the chance.[66]

The same was true of Gypsy bands that frequently wandered around the area. At times, 50 to 100 nomadic Gypsies or Kalmucks would camp near a colony in large numbers and set up their tents. They might stay the winter there. They went about as beggars in the daytime in the villages and stole everything that was easy to take. At night, they would come back and steal the items that they had spotted in the daytime. When they had any chance, they drove away the cattle and sometimes stole even children who their parents never saw again.

Artist Drawing of Kalmucks [67]

Chapter 5
Downright Ugly
Don Cossack Emelian Pugachev

Ural Cossack

Emelian Ivanovich Pugachev was born in a Don Cossack town along the Don River in 1742. [68] He was the son of a small landowner.[69] The Don Cossacks were settlers who in the 1500's founded the almost independent republic of the Don Cossacks on the fertile steppes along the lower course of the Don River.[70] Cossack's became military mercenaries used by the Russian government to quell uprisings and fight battles. For their service and loyalty to the Russian government, they were given special privileges including the opportunity to govern themselves. The Cossack's practiced social and political equality, and elected officials within each community and over the assembly of all communities. [71]

Emelian Ivanovich Pugachev married a young Cossack girl named Sofia Ndeyuzheva. By age 16, he had fought in several wars to include the Seven Years War and the first Russo Turkish War.[72] He served with some distinction in the Russian Army during the Seven Years War[73] and was promoted to Cossack khorunzhiy (junior lieutenant).[74] He returned home, but soon became bored with the slow domestic life. He deserted the Russian Army [75] and chose to wander the area as a frontier adventurer. Pugachev visited the monasteries of the Eastern Orthodox Church and spent much time studying with the Old Believers of the Church. [76]

In the year 1773, a rebellion and uprising broke out in the Volga area led by 33 year old Emelian Ivanovich Pugachev. [77] A drawing of Pugachev, and a photo of a typical Cossack is the previous page.[78] Pugachev took advanyade of a widespread peasant belief that Russian Tsar Peter III had not been murdered. He claimed that he was Tsar Peter III.[79]

Pugachev must have been one of those natural born charismatic leaders. He was able to attract a huge army of Cossacks, serfs, lower class peasants and bandits. He found himself at the head of an army and of a revolutionary movement. He and his "army of freedom" brought cruelty and devastation to the newly founded German settlements.

All of the colonies, except for perhaps those on the Karaman River, appear to have suffered more or less as the rebel army moved from Saratov to Kamyshin along the Astrakhan highway. On August 6, 1774, Pugachev took over the city of Saratov, opened the prisons, the grain storage warehouses, and the salt depots. He also tore down the liquor stores, and let his followers plunder the houses. He hanged all the nobility that he caught and prevented their burial. It was probably while in Saratov that Pugachev heard for the first time about the German settlers in this region.

Emelian Ivanovich Pugachev Campaign map & Area of Rebellion [80]

On August 11, 1774, Pugachev and his Army arrived in the colony village of Donhof and immediately went to Count Donhof''s house. The count's wife, sick in bed, was home alone with a two-month-old child. Pugachev broke into this home and on entering her room, ordered the sick woman to leave her bed immediately. She did not respond fast enough, so he knocked her to the floor. He grabbed the small child and threw it into a corner of the room. He searched the room and stabbed the bed with his dagger to make sure that no one was hiding there. Pugachev was very unhappy with not finding Count Donhof, so he ordered the village to be set on fire, beginning with the house of Count Donhof.

In the colony village of Kratzke, Pugachev erected gallows and hung four people. His army ransacked the houses, struck old men, women and children with whips, but did not kill anyone. By the dawn, a few houses and the granaries had been set on fire were torched, but fortunately the fires did not spread. However, all the livestock was butchered and taken away to feed his rebel army.

During his march through the Volga region, he came to the colony village of Norka and demanded a number of wagons to transport the baggage (plunder) of his army to the next station. As the Pugachev hordes came close to the colonies, everyone did everything they could to save family and property from the rebels. Cellars, sand and clay pits, and even the water wells were filled with all possible property and covered over with earth. Livestock was driven into the forests or were tied up among the reeds along the riverbanks. Almost everyone, even the old people and children, left the village for safety. The army of rabble following Pugachev not only carried out their customary robberies, but also committed murders. Small gangs of agitators and plunderers, who split off from the main rebel group, rode or drove around the villages with impunity, to rob and steal using his name. No one would fight the small groups in fear of bringing down the wrath of Emelian Pugachev.

Eventually near Volgograd, Pugachev and his army of rabble was defeated by a Russian military force led by Russian General Michelson. He fled to hiding deep in the area of the Urals. Defeated by the Russian Army and in hiding, Pugachev's followers lost their faith in their new TSAR. He was deserted and betrayed by his followers, and captured and put in an iron cage. Punishment finally came to Emelian Pugachev as he was in Moscow on January 10, 1775 where he was beheaded, quartered, and burned.[81] This was the end of Pugachev and his rebellion. When he and his band were captured over 430 Volga Germans were found to be members of his army. They were also punished.[82] This is a drawing of Pugachev behind bars. [83]

Emelian Pugachev caused unbelievable suffering for the Volga Germans. The pillaging, rapes, and murders performed by the army under his control was all for nothing but a grab for power. While his grudge was with Catherine the Great and the Tsarist rule, it was the common people that he punished. The German-Russians of the Volga Colonies considered him nothing more than a bandit and murderer. Ironically, there are Russian historians that now consider him to have been a peasant leader in the fight for the emancipation of the Russian serf.[84] He is a "hero" to some and his memory lives on in folk songs and ballads.[85] Others consider him an important part of the birth of Russian Socialism.[86] Something like a "necessary evil" in the evolution of Socialist Government. The Soviet Government renamed the town that he was born to "Pugachev" in his honor, and there are central squares in Russia also named in honor of him.[87]

Below is a painting from 1875, or 100 years after his march of terror. It is titles *"Pugachev's Judgement*" and shows Pugachev holding "court" with his followers. The painting appears to portray that he was a legitimate leader of a respectable people, and not a robber and murderer leading a band of terrorists.

Pugachev's Judgement [88]

Chapter 6
More Downright Ugly
LENIN & the RED GUARDS

With the beginning of the First World War, the situation for the German-Russians changed suddenly. The war led to a deterioration of relations with the German-Russians. Despite the fact that the Volga German-Russians were loyal to the Russian realm, the Russian Government did not trust them and issued measures to control them. German-Russian soldiers in the Russian Army were withdrawn from the western front near Germany and instead used to the fight against Turkey.

The Russian government adopted two laws in 1915. They were called "liquidation laws", because both aimed at the base of life of the German settlers, the ownership of land. The first law determined that all persons of German, Austrian and Hungarian nationality, who had become Russian citizens after 1 January 1880 in a zone of 150 Werst along the border to Germany and Austria Hungary as well as in a zone of 100 Werst along the coast of Baltic Sea, Black Sea, and Asov Sea, must sell their land their landed property within ten to sixteen months to someone still eligible to own property. Persons that were of the Orthodox Faith or those that renounced their religion and switched to the Orthodox Faith were able to keep their land and own even more. World War I turned the Russian people totally against the Volga Germans.

The conversion law of January 1917 dissolved the Volga colonies. Deportation was planned for February 1917. A quote from the Bishop of Saratov at that time: "*On February 26,*

1917 there was an order sent out by the Czar demanding of the 2,000,000 German people in Russia, all of their grain and goods and cattle and horses that they had in their possession. Upon the fall of the Czarist government, it was found that this order was planned by the Czarist government with the view to starving and driving all of the German subjects out of the dominion of Russia. At the time of the fall of the Czarist government, orders were in the hands of the army to proceed with forces into the colonies along the Volga to execute this commandeering ukase. On that same day, I had urged the boys in my Seminary of Saratov (because there were no men except old men at home) to pray for a miracle to save us from extinction, and on the same day, the revolution began in Petrograd, 1800 mounted Cossacks were held in readiness at Saratov, to swoop down on the defenseless villages, to murder, plunder and scatter the inhabitants. But on account of the revolution the order was never executed."[89]

The Bolshevik Revolution and following violent civil war stopped the deportation. The provisional government switched to the Orthodox Faith. The provisional government fell, and the Communists ruled. Working with-in Communist Party Soviet rule, the Volga Germans gained some rights and autonomy as non-Russian minorities.[90] Following the Bolshevik Revolution, the Volga settlements were forced to give up their seed wheat.[91] About 170,000 men, women, and children died of starvation in the German colonies alone.

The Government of Lenin was one of devastation and death. His "subculture of massacre" extended to all areas of Russian control, and the Volga area did not escape. While Lenin did not personally order each execution or mass murder, he did install and use the Soviet system of terror. Some estimate that between 1915 and 1949, about one million German-Russians needlessly perished under the last Russian Tsar, Lenin and Stalin.

The first colony to suffer was Balzer. The Red Guards attacked it in December 1917. After this Government supported attack, there was no safe place for the people. Roving gangs of soldiers and criminals used the Red Guards attack as their authority to prey on the people. Sometime later, the colony of Katharinenstadt was attacked by a hundred Russian soldiers who extorted large sums of money from the villagers before they left.

On Sunday, April 17, 1918, the Red Guards attacked the colony of Schaffhausen while most townspeople were in church. While the townspeople at first succeeded in driving the Red Guard back, the Russians eventually returned with a larger force and seized the town. To make an example, they killed many of the townspeople and drove off most of the livestock.[92]

On July 28, 1918, Lenin issued a decree that established a Commissariat for German Affairs in Saratov. The main responsibility of the Commissariat was to battle the big farmers and the counter-revolutionaries among the Volga Germans. The Commissariat was also to oversee all requisitions in the area. In reality, he was there to direct the terrorizing of the Volga Germans.

In the late summer of 1918, there was a horrible attack on the village of Dobrinka.[93] Three hundred fifty-three German Lutherans founded the village, one of the mother colonies, on June 29, 1764. It was located on the 'Bergseite" (hilly side) or Volga River west bank, south-southwest of Saratov.[94] The historical records tell that the village was attacked and the population robbed. Those that refused to give up their possessions were shot down. Women and children "were raped by the cruel beasts" with several children having died as a result. The records do not specifically say who was responsible for this attack, but they do lead to speculation that the attack was incited by, if not sponsored or sanctioned by, the Commissariat for German Affairs in Saratov.

More importantly, it appears that both the international community and the Volga German-Russians in the area also believed that the Dobrinka attack was Government sponsored.

In September 1918, a diplomatic group from Switzerland, Denmark, and other neutral states protested to the Soviet government about the government sponsored repression and extermination of persons whose only crime was that of belonging to the middle classes.

The Soviet Government's response was: *"(W)e are engaged in a civil war......This counterrevolutionary clique which utilizes foreign and Russian capital to force slavery and war on the Russian people, this clique of Russian workers will ruthlessly annihilate.......(A)gainst our enemies a ruthless war!.... (V)iolence in Russia is used only in the holy interests for the liberation of the masses......"*[95]

Rebellion in Warenburg

Whether it was because the Volga German-Russians were enraged about the attack on their countrymen in Dobrinka, or that all their pastors were sent to slave camps, or that their young men were being drafted for military duty, or for some other action is not really known; for whatever reason the people of Warenburg finally said "NO" in January 1919.

The following is a translation by Richard Kisling. This article appeared on page 5 in the August 26, 1920 issue of Die Welt Post with the title "Hochwichtige Kriegserfahrungen der Wolga-Deutschen" or "Highly Important War Experiences of the Volga Germans". That publication gave credit for the article to the May 15, 1920 issue of Heimkehr, a publication from Germany. Note that it appears to be written with a Russian slant or perspective:

UPRISING IN WARENBURG

"A few months ago we received the first reports about a revolt in the large German colony of Warenburg on the Bergseite [sic]2 of the Volga River. We are now in a position to inform our readers of the details about the events in Warenburg. Pastor Schoening graciously placed the information at our disposal for publication. It was supplemented by statements from persons who recently came out of Russia.

The bodyguard of the present Russian government, known as the Red Army, originally consisted exclusively of volunteers. With the further expansion of the Revolution on the borders of the empire in Siberia, the Ukraine, Poland, Lithuania and the Baltic (in which the [World War I] allies soon took part), the formation of a huge army became imperative. The government was forced to draft non-volunteers into the army and to order a general mobilization. First, in the late autumn of 1918, all of the former officers, noncommissioned officers and sergeants were called up.

Many of these sought to escape but finally had to report, because the government threatened to retaliate against their close relatives. The general mobilization was implemented gradually by province and age group. As early as the autumn of 1918, several age groups were mobilized on the Bergseite of the Province of Saratov, which had precipitated uprisings in several German colonies. The German colonies in Samara Province [Wiesenseite] were especially known to the government as a counterrevolutionary element; as a result they delayed the execution of the mobilization decree until January 1919. All men between the ages of 18 and 45 were to be drafted.

*T*his news reached Warenburg on January 3. The local soviet made the mandate of the Saratov German Bolshevik Commissariat known to the community at a town meeting. Those who attended were seized with deep indignation. Warenburg's soldiers gathered together and, after considering and discussing the situation, unanimously resolved not to follow the command of the commissariat.

*T*hey made a solemn vow to each other to stand together to the end. An action committee of three people was elected. The leaders of the village council reported this occurrence to the district soviet in Seelmann (Rovnoye) and requested a dispatch of a unit of the Red Guard to carry out the mobilization. Seventeen Red Guards were sent from Seelmann, two of whom had originally come from Warenburg.

*T*he insurgents found out in time and met the Red Guards with a squad of twelve men, with Peter Kaiser at their head. The two groups met outside the village. The Red Guards threatened to shoot. The colonists were equipped only with various farm implements; by that time all weapons had long been confiscated. They seized upon a trick and announced to the Reds that they were armed with bombs and would use them immediately.

*T*he Reds, thus intimidated, were taken prisoner. They delivered up a machine gun with five chests of ammunition, sixteen rifles and over two thousand rounds of ammunition. Then they were locked up in Warenburg. Five of them, who had voluntarily entered the Red Guard, were killed by the enraged farmers on the way back to the village. In the meantime, the leadership of the local village soviet had telegraphed to Balzer (a nearby village) and asked for help. The commissariat there sent thirty-eight men, all volunteers and on horseback, under the leadership of the teacher, Schaufler.

On January 5 at 10 a.m., this unit approached the village. It had come by way of Achmat and Lauve. As a precaution, Schaufler stayed behind in the latter village. The insurgents were forewarned by the sentinels they had established. In the square in front of the church, they set up the machine gun they had captured the previous day.

As the Reds approached, a shot rang out from their midst. This was the signal for the Warenburgers to attack. They aimed the machine gun at the approaching Red Guards and mowed them all down. Only three wounded [Reds] escaped, and they spread the news of the uprising everywhere. Among the seriously wounded there was even a capitalist, who had joined the Bolshevik army in order to thus save his

wealth, but he died of his wounds.

The incidents in Warenburg were telegraphed via Achmat and Balzer to Saratov. The captured material this time amounted to: one machine gun with five cases of munitions; thirty to forty rifles with rounds of ammunition; hand grenades, revolvers and swords.

A regiment stationed in Saratov and made up of Latvians, Russians and Hungarians was sent to Warenburg on a retaliatory mission. The Warenburgers had already received news about this and had quickly organized battle preparations. There were, in addition, two hundred men from the *neighboring village of Preuss, who had arrived ready to help, armed with rifles and agricultural equipment. Both machine guns were set up in Warenburg, and the side streets were blockaded with harrows and other implements.*

At 9 o'clock the militia from Saratov arrived. Upon their arrival in the village, fire opened up from both sides. There were many dead and wounded on the side of the Reds. They had to pull back and continued the bombardment in front of the village. The gunfire lasted all day and into the night. Because it was frightfully cold, that is to say 26 degrees Reaumur [sic]3, they pulled back by degrees to the nearest villages. Following this, the night remained calm for the most part.

The next morning at 7 o'clock, the news spread that a regiment of support troops from Pokrovsk [Engels] was advancing with three field guns (cannons). Simultaneous with the arrival of the Pokrovsk troops, eighty-six men from the German Commissariat in Saratov also appeared. The Warenburgers saw that they were no match for this superior power; their will to resist weakened. The auxiliaries from neighboring Preuss marched off in view of this event. The position of the Warenburgers became untenable.

The Reds sent in an emissary right away that same morning at about 10 o'clock to ask whether or not the Warenburgers would surrender. The farmers wanted peace, which was assured them with the surrender of all of their weapons. At that point, the aforementioned regiment advanced into the village, which was already surrounded by troops.

After the [Red] prisoners, about ninety men, were freed by the Latvian regiment, the commander said, "Now we'll show them!" That was the signal for general plundering. All who had taken part in the uprising were taken prisoner. Seven men were shot immediately. About ninety men were killed in all. On Wednesday, January 8, Schutz, the investigating magistrate, came from Saratov, and the terrible trial began.

All who were under suspicion of participating in the uprising in any way were brought forth. About thirty men were placed on the mountain slope of the village and likewise shot. All their possessions were confiscated. The wives and children of those involved had to leave their homes just as they were. Homeless in the middle of winter, they sought shelter with friends and relatives.

Damages of 1,300,000 rubles were levied against the colony. The sum that each had to pay individually was specified. Anyone who refused or could not raise the money was to be shot. The retribution was paid in two hours. About four to five million rubles were confiscated. The worst treatment was to those who had Schutzscheine [certificates of protection] from the German Empire. Five who had been sentenced to death escaped.

A bounty of 10,000 [rubles] was placed on their heads. The systematic plundering of the village continued all that day and the following day. Many sheep, 380 horses, nearly 200 cows, camels and other livestock, poultry, food supplies and clothing were expropriated.

One of the fugitives, Wormsbecher, who had been at the head of the insurrection, was discovered and brought in on the 10th. He was terribly mistreated on the way back to the village, with a rope around his neck tied to a sled, which he had to run along beside. He was to be hanged immediately. Wormsbecher was hanged on the large church square.

We further excerpt from the German [language] newspaper *Nachrichten*, the communist organ published in Saratov, the official account of the uprising.

Record of the Special Investigation Commission

Those present were Comrades Saranzev, Ostroglasov, Ebenholz, Schoenfeld, Alfred Schutz, Eduard Schutz, Johann Zitzer and Schulz Grab. Individuals were named with the distribution of duties: as Commander of all Troops Present and President of the Collegium, Comrade Nachalov and Comrade Ebenholz; as Investigative magistrates, the Comrades Eduard Schutz and Hermann Schutz; Director in Charge of Arrests, Comrade Zitzer; Deputy President, Comrade Schoenfeld; Administrator of Finances, Comrade Reichert; Commander of Those Arrested, Comrade Ostroglasov; Secretary, Alfred Schutz.

Because of their active participation in the uprising [the following men] were judged and condemned to death by shooting:

Heinrich Trippel, Friedrich Hammel, Alexander Hart, Georg Kraft, Heinrich Gabel (Goebel), Philipp Hubert, Georg Werner, Konrad Roth, August Kramer, Heinrich Roth, Heinrich Hartwig, Philipp Pfeifer, Andreas Eisner, Heinrich Michael Hartwig, David Schutz, Alexander Pfeiffer, Johann Schutz, Heinrich Schutz, Johann Pfeiffer, Jacob Rasch, Philipp Adolf, Friedrich

Schmal, Heinrich Bier, Eduard Simon, Philipp Becker, Heinrich Schpomer (Spomer), Philipp Schpomer (Spomer), Johann Braun, Friedrich Simon, Heinrich Eisener (Eisner), Johann Stamm, Jaeger Wagenleiter (Wagenleitner), Michael Funkner, and Heinrich Stuppel.

Others who were convicted (but escaped):Friedrich Klein, Philipp Doering, Peter Kaiser (father), Peter Kaiser (son), Friedrich Krikau, and Peter Schmidt.

The death sentences were carried out right after the arrests. The property of the condemned was confiscated, as was the property of Vladimir Wormsbecher, whose wife and children were able to keep only the absolute necessities, while the remainder was given over to the Committee for the Poor. The assessment of 1,300,000 rubles, which was imposed on Warenburg, was apportioned in the following manner: Friedrich Schmall, 50,000 [rubles]; Alexander Bier, 50,000; and so on."[96]

This "uprising" was obviously an act of desperation. Whatever the reason, it ended badly for the colony of Warenburg. The rebellion accomplished nothing. The the number of those who became homeless and were left without protection was beyond counting.[97]

My Grandparents and Great-Grandparents left Warenburg from 1895-1913, not very many years before the 1919 uprising. It is probable that at least some of the men involved were probably distant cousins. The census records for that time have not been made available yet, but I would guess that the names listed below were at least distantly related to me:

Philipp Adolf	**Philipp Becker**
Peter Kaiser (father)	**Peter Kaiser (son)**
August Kramer	**Heinrich Roth**

Konrad Roth

Peter Schmidt

David Schutz

Johann Schutz

Heinrich Schutz

Eduard Simon

Friedrich Simon

Heinrich Trippel

Georg Werner

Chapter 7
The Worst
of the Downright Ugly

If the weather, the bandits, the wild Natives, Pugachev, and Lenin and the Red Guards were not enough, there was also the grossly inefficient Russian Government bureaucracy to add to the colonists' pain. Combine all these, and you have the recipe for **Famine**.

Famine

Famine is defined in one of my dictionaries as "an extreme scarcity of food, starvation," etc.[98] With all the food produced, it is hard to believe that people do starve to death. However, even today, the headlines are full of areas that still suffer from famines. What caused the famines in the long past Medieval Germany, and in the 1800's and 1900's in Russia, is the subject of this chapter.

Famine in Medieval Germany

Famine was a familiar occurrence back in earlier time in Medieval Germany and Europe. Any famine in Medieval Europe meant that people died of starvation on an unbelievable scale. Localized famines occurred in Europe during the 14th century in 1304, 1305, 1310, 1315-1317 (the Great Famine), 1330-1334, 1349-1351, 1358-1360, 1371, 1374-1375 and 1390. For most families there was usually never enough to eat and life was day-to-day. Refrigeration of food was not yet possible and fresh food had to be acquired every day. Because of this, life was a relatively short and was a brutal struggle to survive to old age. Old age could be 30 years old.

Official records of the British Royal family tell us that the average life expectancy in 1276 was about 35 years. Between 1301 and 1325 during the Great Famine, it was lower at 30 years. Even worse, during the Black Death (1348-1375) it plummeted to a little more than 17 years. The 1315 to 1317 Great Famine was limited to Northern Europe. This area extended from Russia in the east to Ireland in the west, from Scandinavia in the north and bounded in the south by the Alps and the Pyrenees. Note that Germany was right in the middle. The coming of the Great Famine had been unnoticed in the changing weather patterns for decades. The yield ratios of wheat had been dropping since 1280 and food prices had been steadily climbing.[99]

Apparently, the cause of this was the changing of the weather. Sometime around 1280, a European wide cooling event began which lasted until the 19th century. It is now known as "The Little Ice Age". The Little Ice Age (LIA) cooling ended an unusually warm era known as the Medieval climate optimum. There were three cycles, beginning about 1650, about 1770, and 1850, each separated by slight warming intervals. The Little Ice Age was world-wide, but is most thoroughly documented in Europe and North America. Glaciers in the Swiss Alps that had been retreating for eons began to advance, engulfing farms and crushing entire villages.

The River Thames and the canals and rivers of the Netherlands often froze over during the winter, and people skated and even held frost fairs on the ice. It would not be until much later that climatologists would realize that the Medieval Warm Period (MWP) or Medieval Climate Optimum that Europe had come to view as normal was actually an unusually warm period lasting from about the 10th century to about the 14th century. This is when Europe and Germany agriculturally prospered, with the subsequent tremendous population increase. Now we know that a better name for this warming would have been "the Medieval Climatic Anomaly". With the on-set of colder weather, the future of farming and food production would be seriously affected.[100] As noted above, during this "Medieval Warm Period" the population of Europe had increased tremendously, reaching levels that were not reached again in some areas until the 19th century. Changing weather patterns, governments unable to do anything about the weather (much like now), and a spiraling population level to a historical high made it a time ripe for disaster.

The Great Famine began in spring 1315. Unusually heavy rain covered much of Europe. This rain and cool temperatures continued thru spring and summer. With too much moisture and little or no sun, grain could not ripen outside, and it was brought indoors in urns and pots. The straw and hay for the animals feed could not be cured; with the result that there was a shortage of livestock feed. The price of food began to rise. Since refrigeration was not developed yet, salting of the food was mandatory as it was the only way to cure and preserve the meat. But salt became difficult to obtain because it could not be evaporated in the wet weather, and the price shot up making it too expensive for most people. As the rains continued, wheat prices grew by 320 percent making bread unaffordable to peasants. Any long term emergency stores of grain were kept by the lords and nobles for their own survival. People began to harvest wild edible roots, plants, grasses, nuts, and bark in the forests. The spring of 1316 arrived, and it continued to rain.

The general European population was deprived of food for so long that it was no longer able to sustain itself. All classes of society from the nobles to peasants were affected, but the peasants were hurt the worst. The peasants represented 95% of the population and had no food reserves. Starving people did what they had to do, and slaughtered the draft animals, and ate the seed grapes. This would all affect their agricultural future. Children were abandoned by parents, while at the same time old people voluntarily refused food in hopes of that the younger generation would live. Rumors of many incidents of cannibalism were recorded. The year 1317 arrives and the wet weather continues. Finally in the summer of 1317 the weather returned to its normal patterns. However by now thousands of people were weakened by diseases such as pneumonia, bronchitis, tuberculosis, and other sicknesses. Almost all the seed stock had been eaten. It was not until around 1325 that the food supply returned to near normal conditions. It is estimated that between 10%-25% of the population of many cities and towns died. While the "Black Death" of 1338-1375 would kill more, for many the Great Famine was worse. While the plague might run through an area in a matter of months, the effect of the Great Famine lingered for many years.

This particular famine is called the Great Famine not only because of the number of people who died, or the vast geographic area that was affected, or the length of time it lasted, but also because of the lasting consequences. The first consequence was for Religion. No amount of prayer appeared effective against the causes of the famine. Remember, this was a time where the final recourse to all problems had been religion. Religion prescribed prayer, and no amount of prayer seemed to help. This negatively affected the faith of the starving population with the resulting undermining of the institutional authority of the Church.

The second consequence was the increase in criminal activity. Europe in the 13th century had already been a violent culture where rape and murder were common occurrences.

Starving people will do almost anything to survive, and even "good people" were forced to violate the rules of society. Following the famine, Europe became a tougher and more violent world. Third was the inability of the governments to deal with the crisis. As far as the people were concerned, Church and God seemed unable or unwilling to answer prayers, and their earthly leaders and Kings were equally ineffective. This weakened and undermined both Church and King power and authority. The Great Famine also marked a clear end to the unprecedented period of population growth that had started around 1050. The population health was so weakened that while there now was available food, the next great calamity (the Black Death) was just around the corner.[101]

Russian Famine Years 1891-1892

In 1891 thru 1892, a famine hit Russia. This was not the first famine in Russia. The Nikonian Chronicle, written between 1127 and 1303, listed eleven famine years in Russia during that time. Russian Tsar Alexander I was the first Russian Monarch to attempt to create a comprehensive famine relief system in 1822. This program was modified by Tsar Nicholas I in 1834, and provided for a network of granaries. The idea was that the peasants should stock up in good years and then empty out during a crop failure. While this theory looked good on paper, in practice it was a complete failure. Even in the best years the peasants were too poor to contribute, and where the granaries actually existed they were usually empty. History also records a famine in the year 1873 when Leo Tolstoy became aware of the seriousness of a famine in Samara when he was visiting his estate there.

The famine of 1891-1892 was particularly bad. It affected the population of an area of around 900,000 square miles in the Volga and central agricultural areas. These were the most fertile and productive parts of Russia, and included the provinces of Nizhni-Novgorod, Riazan, Tula, Kazan, Simbirsk, Saratov, Penza, Samara and Tambov. The famine came about partially because of a recent past of poor harvests (6 of the last 12 years). Between the years of 1879 and 1889, six of the years saw poor harvests. These harvests had been negatively affected by both natural problems and by man-made circumstances (drought, population growth, poor growing seasons, and soil erosion).

The dry autumn of 1891 delayed the seeding of the fields. The winter began early and was more severe than usual with only light snowfall. Heavy snow usually protects the seedlings from the cold. Normally, melting snow and ice would cause spring floods of the Volga that would spread over the plains whose grass is used as fodder for the animals. The small amount of snow this year only caused the ground to freeze. The freezing killed the young plants because the delayed seeding and late planting did not give new plants enough time to take root. The bad weather eliminated the main source of feed for the animals. The animal's health was crucial to the peasants because they provided the power needed to plow the fields. The cold weather lasted until mid-April. The summer of 1892 was extremely hot and dry with five rainless months. This resulted in the smallest total grain harvest for European Russia in a decade.

It was also caused by man-made circumstances that lead to less food production in farming areas and increased export of what was grown. In 1891 Russia was going through a social shift in rural areas were the number of small farms was reduced while larger farms were increased. The larger estates tended to grow products for foreign export to earn cash. This was farm collectivization driven by financial factors. The result was that the total amount of food grown in Russia had declined while the amount of exports increased. This change, along with several poor harvests in a short period, made the area susceptible to famine.

This famine was at its worst in Ukraine and the Volga region. Local authorities were hesitant to report the famine as they would look bad. The problem remained hidden while the people starved. When the central government did learn of the famine, it was also reluctant to acknowledge the famine as it would look bad. And there was the idea that the central government mandated shift of farmers from small plots to large farms was a major contributing factor to the famine's outbreak. Even after the famine was public knowledge, the government mandated export of food products from the famine area to overseas markets continued. This caused more and more people to die. On the positive side, it also brought more funds into the central government treasury.

Count Leo Tolstoy was a vocal critic of the government, and blamed it for its policies regarding the famine itself. He also criticized the relief efforts implemented by the state. He felt the government had not understood the true causes of the famine, they did not know what was really going on in the famine area, and mishandled relief efforts. Tolstoy wanted the government to gather accurate statistics by sending officials into the villages to compile from individual inquiries the data needed for wise and efficient aid.[102] Tolstoy also claimed that the government provided no help for laborers who were able to work, and for those with horses or cattle. He reported that large quantities of grain were either stolen or allowed to spoil, thus wasting precious food and money. Tolstoy suggested the construction of large-scale public works, the regulation of grain, and forbidding the hoarding of flour. He also supported the opening of sufficient free eating-houses in famine villages along with the organization of all available voluntary forces in national relief work. The Russian Government in St. Petersburg ignored his suggestions.

Not satisfied with this, Tolstoy left Yasnaya Polyana and went to his estate in the Dankovsky district. There he gathered information on the needs of each family and individual. He set up eating rooms of his own that provided two meals a day and a supply of wood for fuel during the winter in exchange for work. For those unable to work and the neediest, it was free. At the same time, his wife was collecting donations for his work in Moscow. Tolstoy and his wife opened soup booths in twenty-two villages, and set up corn and clothing stores for those suffering.[103] Tolstoy also made sure that horses and work materials were supplied to the people in order to help them to make their own clothes and shoes. He bought the surplus goods at full price and distributed them among the poorest people. To prevent a repetition of the famine, he provided seed and replaced horses so the peasants would be able to plant and prepare for the next harvest.[104] He remained in the famine areas until after the good harvest of 1893, which brought the territory back to normal.

As for the Russian Government, they did finally order that grain would no longer be exported or shipped overseas in November 1891. By this time graphic details of the suffering in the famine areas began circulating in the West with reports dealing with the famine containing as much detail as possible. Even then, the Russian Government refused to acknowledge the scope of the problem and/or accept aid from outside. In 1892, the Russian government did eventually accept foreign charitable assistance and so many lives were saved.

There were also major relief efforts from the United States and other western countries that sent grain and money to the beleaguered area. Western newspapers sent correspondents into the area to report on the situation first hand. They described in extreme detail the horrors they saw, and pleaded for their readers to contribute to the relief effort to help the starving. The Iowa Auxiliary of the Red Cross sent a shipment of corn instead of money because the reporters had described how inefficiently the aid was getting to the peasants. [105]

Sympathetic Philadelphians sent six million pounds of flour that had been collected by merchant millers. The publisher of Northwestern Miller, W.C. Edgar, who assembled a donation collected from states, started this relief. Transportation was provided free of charge by railroads and sent on two steamships from New York to the Baltic port of Libau. Mr. Edgar accompanied the expedition, wrote articles about the situation, and encouraged others to help in the relief. [106]

One of the largest relief campaigns in Russian history was undertaken by the government to help alleviate the disaster in which eleven million people received supplemental rations from the state. As Tolstoy had observed and written, the famine proved that the tsarist government was inept and inefficient in a way that made it incapable of foreseeing the disaster. It also mishandled the relief effort in spite of the tremendous effort that was undertaken.

The Russian famine focused attention on the internal weakness and utter backwardness of the Russian Empire. This is not to say that they did nothing. Tsar Alexander III organized a special Relief Committee. He named the Caesarovich, the future Nicholas II, as president. The Emperor himself gave around five million rubles to relief funds while his Empress collected twelve million rubles from foreign donations for the famine areas. The Empress' sister, Grand Duchess Elizabeth, organized her own relief committee that held bazaars in Moscow to sell peasant-made items. Unfortunately, the central treasury with its slow cumbersome procedures was the main source of famine relief funds. For this reason, aid was extremely slow in getting to those needing it. Compounding this was the lack of adequate transportation or a distribution network. The government distributed special financial aid of 150 million rubles to the people to finance food and seed purchases. They bought food, then loaned it to those who could be expected to repay. However, the ability to repay made only some workers and landowners eligible. This left the rest of the rural population consisting of the elderly, children, and widows excluded.[107]

Flour was distributed monthly to children over the age of two and to those unable to work. The amount given out would only last between fifteen to twenty days. Due to the lack of fuel, it usually had to be eaten raw. Many were denied aid because the government hoped that they would find work. The government in St. Petersburg did not understand that there was no work to be found.[108] As usual in these times, the power of the official to choose who received food and who did not (practically deciding who lived and who died) was very often abused. Only one-third of the seed that was needed was distributed. Much of what was distributed was eaten instead of being planted. Even if enough seed had been provided most of the peasants would have been unable to plow because millions of horses either died or were sold. This left enormous areas of productive land unsown.

In February 1892, the government addressed the shortage of stock problem by arranging for the purchase of 30,000 horses from the Kirghiz steppes. With all this, the total number of deaths due to the famine of 1891-1892 was approximately 700,000.[109] Even worse, this famine affected the lives of between fourteen to twenty million people.

Another Famine Arrives

Many of the agricultural harvests from the years 1915 to 1931 were negatively affected because of WWI, the Russian Civil War and the constantly changing agricultural policies of the new Communist government. In the fall of 1920 and 1921, widespread total crop failures occurred along the Volga River, and another great famine plagued the area.[110] During this time, about one third of the population[111] or 166,000 Volga German-Russians starved to death because of a famine caused by weather, collective farming, and political purges[112]. Many felt that The Russian government was responsible for these deaths since the Bolshevistic government allowed the international community to help these victims of famine only after over 100,000 had lost their lives. 1920 was a drought year, but the German farmers had learned from the years of living in the Volga region of the absolute requirement to store up enough food to last at least two years. The government took away this complete stockpile of food by means of requisitioning bands. With no reserves left, the famine was inevitable.[113]

MOVING THE BODIES

In the early spring of 1921, the Volga area people worked the extremely rich "Black Earth" under clear skies. When light winter snows finally ended, hot weather settled in. When the time came for the farmers go to plow and sow their fields, all they found was dry, cracked mud. They plowed and sowed their seed anyway, and prayed for rain. It did not come. The Russian Famine that began in 1921 and ended in the summer of 1923, was one of the worst disasters in the area's history.[114]

Many formerly prosperous and well off Volga Germans found themselves to be paupers and were forced to become vagabonds and beggars.[115] From Alexandra Rakhmanova's diary August 15, 1921: "The train moves slowly, passing endless evacuation trains from the famine areas of the Volga and the North. The cattle trains are crowded with people, piled up like coal: men, women, children. But are these still people? Many of them lost their teeth, their gums are bleeding, their faces are green and ash-gray."[116] Previous page photo [117]

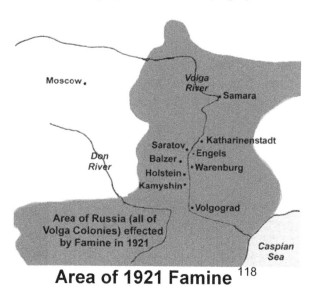

Area of 1921 Famine [118]

Reports of the terrible conditions made the newspaper headlines. One reporter wrote:" *We went down to the shore of the Volga, down a rough broken street, past booths where you could buy white bread, and, not a hundred yards away, found an old woman cooking horse dung in a broken saucepan. Within sight of the market was a mass of refugees, men, women, and children, with such belongings as they had retained in their flight from starvation, still starving, listlessly waiting for the wagons to move them away to more fortunate districts. Some of them are sheltered from the rain that is coming now, too late, by the roofs of open-sided sheds. Others are sitting hopelessly in the open, not attempting to move, not even begging. I shall never forget the wizened dead face, pale green of a silently weeping little girl, whose feet were simply bones over which was stretched dry skin that looked like blue-black leather. And she was one of hundreds. A fortnight ago there were twenty thousand waiting beside the quays of Samara. Every day about 1,400 are taken off in wagons. There are, of course, no latrines. The beach was black with excreta until, as an eye-witness (not a Communist) told me, the local Communists arranged a 'Saturdaying' which deserves a place in history, and themselves removed that disgusting ordure, and, for a day or two, lessened the appalling stench that is beginning once more to rise from the beach.*

In the morning of the second day we called at one of the sixty "children's houses" in Samara, so that Ercole could photograph the famine orphans, the children purposely abandoned in the streets, in the state in which they were received. The garden, a plain courtyard with a few trees, was full of children lying in the sun under the wall, staring in silent unchildlike groups, ragged, half-naked, some with nothing whatever but a shirt. All were scratching themselves. Among these children, a man and a woman were walking about, talking quietly to them, and carrying sick children into the house, bringing others out. Ercole had hardly begun to turn the handles of his machine before some of the children saw us, and, some with fright, some with interest, all scrambled to their feet, although many of them fell again, and, too weak to get up, stayed sitting on the ground where they fell. Ercole photographed them as they were. Then he picked four little boys and photographed these alone. Wishing to reward them, he gave them some chocolate before the woman looking after them had time to stop him. "You must not do it," she said; "they are too hungry." But it was already too late. All of them who had strength to move were on top of each other, fighting for the scraps of chocolate like little animals, with small, weak, animal cries.

That is only one of dozens of such scenes that we witnessed during those two days in Samara. Samara is one place of hundreds. Everywhere people are trying to save the children. Nowhere have they the means that we in other countries have to give what they should be given. And, to the shame of humanity, there are some in Western Europe who have urged that help should not be given. Outside the goods station is a huge camp of white tents, a military camp of the Red Army, handed over bodily by the army authorities for the use of the refugees. The refugees have over-flowed from the tents and built more tents, and wigwams for themselves out of anything that came handy - rags, branches of trees, pieces of old iron from the railway sidings. Everywhere on the open ground outside the cemetery, whither every day fresh bodies are carried ('Thirty-five this morning,' a man told us, whose little hut commanded the entrance to the cemetery), and along the railway line for half a mile or so, were little camp fires, and people cooking scraps of pumpkin rind, scraps of horse-dung, here and there scraps of bread and bits of cabbage. In all that vast crowd there was not one who did not look actually hungry, and for many mere hunger would be a relief.

Among them from tent to tent walked an unshaven young man with a white forage cap, now nearly black, a blue shirt and breeches, and no coat. A mechanic who was carrying the camera tripod for us told me who he was. He was a German, one-time prisoner of war, now a Communist, and 'for all that,' as my man put it, 'a man of God. He has stayed since the beginning. He never leaves them. I don't believe he ever sleeps. Whatever can be got for them he gets it. He has taken and lived through all their diseases. It is owing to that one man that there is such order in this place instead of pandemonium. Thousands owe their very lives to him. If only there were a few more like that.' I wished to speak to that young German, but, just as I was making my way to him through the crowd, a little skeleton of a boy pulled at his sleeve and pointed to a tent behind him. The young man turned aside and disappeared into the tent. As I walked by the tents, even without going into them, the smell of dysentery and sickness turned my stomach like an emetic.

A little crowd was gathered beside a couple of wooden huts in the middle of the camp. I went up there and found that it was a medical station where a couple of doctors and two heroic women lived in the camp itself fighting cholera and typhus. The crowd I had noticed were waiting their turns for vaccination. At first the people had been afraid of it, but already there was no sort of difficulty in persuading them to take at least this precaution, though seemingly nothing will ever teach them to keep clean. The two women brought out a little table covered with a cloth and the usual instruments, and the crowd already forming into a line pressed forward. I called to Ercole and he set up his camera. One of the sisters called out 'Lucky ones to-day; vaccination and having your pictures taken at the same time,' and while the camera worked, those behind urged those in front to be quick in taking their rags off, and to get on so that they too would be in time to come into the picture.

CHILD OF FAMINE

There were old men and women, girls and little ragged children. Shirt after shirt came off, showing ghastly bags of bones, spotted all over with bites and the loathsome scars of disease. And, dreadful as their condition was, almost all showed an interest in the camera, while I could not help reflecting that before the pictures are produced some at least of them will have left the camp and made their last journey into the cemetery over the way, the earth of which, as far as you could see, was raw with new-made graves. Left photo [119]

In the siding beyond the camp was a refugee train, a sort of rolling village, inhabited by people who were for the most part in slightly better condition than the peasants flying at random from the famine. These were part of the returning wave of that flood of miserable folk who fled eastwards before the retreating army in 1915 and 1916, and are now uprooted again and flying westwards again with the whip of hunger behind them. To understand the full difficulty of Samara's problem it is necessary to remember the existence of these people who are now being sent back to the districts or the new States to which they belong. They have prior right to transport, and, in the present condition of Russian transport, the steady shifting of these people westwards still further lessens the means available for moving the immediate victims of the drought. I walked from one end of the train to the other. It was made up of cattle trucks, but these trucks were almost like huts on wheels, for in each one was a definite group of refugees and a sort of family life. These folks had with them their belongings, beds, bedding, chests of drawers, rusty sewing machines, rag dolls. I mention just a few of the things I happened to see. In more than one of the wagons I found three or four generations of a single family - an old man and his still more ancient mother struggling back to the village which they had last seen in flames as it was set on fire by the retreating army, anxious simply, as they said, 'to die at home,' and with them a grandson, with his wife (married here) and their children.

Families that had lost all else retained their samovar, the central symbol of the home, the hearth of these nomads; and I saw people lying on the platform with samovars boiling away beside them that must have come from West of Warsaw and traveled to Siberia and back.

ANOTHER CHILD

In the doorway of one truck I found a little boy, thinner than any child in England shall ever be, I hope, and in his hand was a wooden cage, and in the cage a white mouse, fat, sleek, contented, better off than any other living thing in all that train. There were a man and his wife on the platform outside. I asked them where they were going. 'To Minsk,' said the man, 'those of us who live; the children are dying every day.' I looked back at the little boy, warming his mouse in the sun. The mouse, at least, would be alive at the journey's end."[120] Above photo[121]

Another reporter wrote in early November 1921: "*Saratov, Russia - As one proceeds up the Volga River, the faces of the inhabitants grow thinner, their death lists increase from hunger, malaria and cholera and make the traveler* *involuntarily recall the "black death" which originated here in the Middle Ages. Thus far there has been no emigration from the city of Saratov but there are 50,000 refugees living in squalor about its river front streets. They have flocked in from the country or are waiting transportation westward. An incident typical of the speculation which takes place amid this struggle for life occurred at Uvek, below Saratov, when the man in charge of two food cars of the American Relief Administration told the correspondent that his cars had not been ferried across the river to the village of Pagashusk because the station master wanted either part of the food for himself or a cash tip.*

TO THE FOOD LINES

At this point on the Volga, the first food-begging began. Barefooted children who were huddled together on the lower decks wandered about the steamer knocking on doors and windows and begging bits of bread. An Italian opera singer going to Samara played the piano and sang the finale of Tosca in the grand saloon until a crowd collected and then asked for bread saying he (sic) had none for three days.

At a German colonist town of Baronsk, formerly a grain center where there are dozens of empty transit granaries, it was said that five to ten persons were daily dying of hunger and malaria, and that last year's scanty crop had been requisitioned by the Bolsheviki who had not left enough for seed grain last summer. Bread costs 8,000 rubles a pound there.

At Baronsk also were 16,000 peasant children whose mothers were unable to feed them. The Soviet had requisitioned the best houses to shelter them and was serving soup to them daily. Left photo [122]

Families Fleeing Famine on the banks of the Volga River [123]

At the once wealthy town of Volsk where the smokeless chimneys of the Portland Cement Works stand on the bleak chalk bluffs above the river, the traveler was met with customary complaints of no medicines and no money to buy food. People meeting the steamer offered their home treasures for food or money. There was signs of pitiful attempts to make use of the Volga River water during the rainless summer to irrigate miles of cabbage patches between the low water and high water marks. The market and shops of the town were closed. The only vestige of pre war activity was *at the cathedral where services were held as usual and the vesper bells called to thin-faced people across the triangular square. "When will the Americans come?" queried an old man with a world of anxiety in his voice as he hobbled toward the church door.*"[124]

Between 1920 and 1921, approximately 72,000 people in the Volga Colonies fled their villages towards the western borders of Russia in an attempt to escape the Famine.[125]

Volga Relief Society (A Good Thing)

Family and friends in the United States also received letters from their relatives in Russia describing the terrible conditions. As a result of these letters, relief societies were organized in many different states in which the German-Russians had settled.

The Volga Relief Society helped immensely by feeding 60,000 adults and 75,000 children, and by distributing medicine, shoes, and warm clothing. The various relief societies reprted that German-Russians living in the United States raised approximately one-half million dollars. This was sent to their friends and families still in the Volga area through cash or food and clothing drafts.[126]

The Volga Relief Society was organized in the Zion Congregational Church of Portland, Oregon, on August 11, 1921. Former residents of the colony of Norka who had migrated to America originally formed the Society. About the same time that the Oregon group came about, other groups of concerned Germans in Fresno, California and Lincoln, Nebraska were also meeting to learn what they could do to help.[127] Families in America, especially in Portland, Oregon; Fresno and surrounding towns in California; and Lincoln, Nebraska, donated large sums of money to help save their fellow countrymen in the old homeland.

A series of letters under the heading "The Latest Letters from the Volga Colonies" appeared in the "Die Welt Post." Examples give us a better picture of the times that tell something of this latter period. Excerpts follow:

"Norka, 15 March 1922

. . . On the dark wretched background of the world political situation, the actions of the American Relief Association rise as a shining star. And that applies also to the Volga Relief Society in less measure. It should remain for all time unforgettable here in the Volga Colonies, what you former sons and daughters in America have done for the old homeland during this terrible time. . . .

Adults starve daily, children no more in the villages where the American food kitchens to some extent could function normally. There is much criticism of the kitchens. But when one asks the critic, "What if the kitchens would not exist?" Then one receives the answer, "We would have several hundred more children's graves here in Norka." And how many children who no longer laugh and no longer cry. It is a heavy sorrow when people can no longer laugh, but it is still more dreadful when want brings people so far that they can no longer cry. Such dulled inhuman pitiable ones are seen here almost every day. . .

Direct help which friends can give friend are the "Food Drafts." . . . Sadly, also here our transportation is to blame that things don't arrive quickly enough. But what luck and joy these $10 food packages provide, which in Russian pounds contain some 53 lbs. flour, 262 lbs. rice, 10 lbs. fat or 9 lbs. bacon, about 11 lbs. sugar, 3 1/2 lbs. tea and 20 cans of milk. After weeks or months that some have received letters that Food

Drafts have been paid, finally comes the distribution notice. All the lucky receivers of such notices gather together and drive to Saratov, where they receive their packages at the A.R.A. warehouse. . . .

What did one not use as substitute tea: There were apple leaves, cherry leaves, dried and roasted pumpkin peels or carrots. Now there is again good tasting tea with sugar in it. One must know the years of deprivation of our country, in order to understand the joy of the precious contents of this package. . . . If one were to give someone here 10 dollars (10 million Rubel) he could buy only half of what he could receive in such a packet. . . . Reverend F. Wacker, Norka Pastor."[128]

By August 1922, the American Relief Association in the Saratov Volga area was feeding approximately one million adults and children each day.[129] Historians have described the 1921-1923 Famine relief work along the Volga River as the most outstanding act of charity ever performed by the German-Russians now living in the United States.[130]

"America to the starving people of Russia" [131]

"Gift of the American people" [132]

It is estimated that anywhere from 2 to 10 million Russians perished from starvation and disease during this period – many more than the 400,000 deaths of the previous major famine of 1891-1892. The droughts of 1921 and 1922 extended over a larger area of Russia than any previous famines, yet that alone does not explain this famine's lethality.

The mass starvation from 1921 to 1924 was largely caused by a government policy of forced grain requisition. When the Volga German-Russians resisted, they were completely stripped of all grain and mass executions were carried out. It is estimated that over thirty percent of the Volga German population was deliberately starved before any relief was permitted. [133]

First Lenin, then Stalin

By 1921 the Civil War in Russia had been settled. Lenin had solidified his power as Communist Party Leader, but Stalin was waiting in the shadows as General Secretary of the Communist Party. Lenin wanted Stalin out.[134] He also supported the creation of the Volga German Autonomous Soviet Socialist Republic in January 1924. This new Republic was made up of 66% Germans, 20% Russians, and 12% Ukrainians.[135] However, on January 21, 1924, Lenin died and a "new sheriff was in town".

Joseph Stalin came to power. The most notable historical accomplishment of Stalin was that he was responsible for the deaths of at least 25 million Russians and minorities (including Volga German-Russians) in Russia. [136]

In 1928, Stalin launched his first five-year plan to boost industrialization in the Soviet Union. The plan was to double steel output and triple both pig iron and tractor production within five years. The money for industrialization was to come from agricultural with the use of collective farms. His aim was to create modern 'socialist agro-towns' that would produce greatly increased yields.

Stalin's collectivization plan began in 1929 and was violent and brutal. Overnight with no warning, small peasant holdings were merged into giant farm collectives of as large as 247,000 acres. Wages were abolished. Workers were paid thru a system of work points that were a share of the collective's output.

As expected, the peasants formed armed rebellions and violently resisted Stalin's plan. They even destroyed their own crops and livestock so that it would not fall into the Government's hands. Stalin's response was extremely severe.

All collective land, agricultural produce and implements were declared to now be state property. Anyone guilty of destroying or damaging them was to be shown no mercy. Peasants were forbidden to leave the countryside without Government permission. Rich peasants (kulaks) were either killed or sent to labor camps. Farming yields fell by 40 per cent. Even so, the forcible seizure of grain was re-introduced and the Soviet Union doubled grain exports.[137]

Famine Again

The peasants remaining in the villages were directed to provide to the Government huge amounts of grain that they were unable to produce.[138] The food shortages were worst in the Soviet Union's richest grain-growing areas, including the Ukraine and Middle Volga. Stalin initiated a campaign to crush Ukrainian nationalism and the rebellious Cossacks, who truthfully reported the existence of famine.

In 1931, Stalin allowed relief grain to be delivered to all regions except the Ukraine.[139] There was enough grain, but it was taken away to the last kilogram. As recent Soviet accounts put it, "this famine was organized by Stalin quite consciously, and according to the plan."[140]

Stalin had realized early the possible potential benefits of a famine. He decided he could use a famine to crush the Ukrainian and German-Russian Volga nationalism. Both groups had become more powerful and assertive about their cultural and political independence.

Stalin was not going to allow this to continue, as this opposed communism and his power. The center of power of both groups was the peasant.[141] Stalin reasoned that destroy the peasants, and collectivization would easily follow.

So in 1932, Stalin put in motion a new tactic where he directed an impossible grain delivery target of 7.7 million tons. Eventually, he reduced it to 6.6 million tons. One survivor was quoted as saying, "*Our village was given a quota that it couldn't have fulfilled in ten years!*"

The quotas were a sentence to death by starvation for all the peasant families. His war strategy was simple: to force the unwilling peasants into communes, while also destroying the spiritual resources and cultural achievements that supported their nationalism.[142] If they would not go to communes, they could just die.

Stalin and the Communist Party showed the starving peasants no mercy. The Party used detachments of workers and activists to seize every last bit of produce or grain, including the seed grain needed for planting. They searched through peasant homes with rods, breaking into walls and ceilings for hidden stores of food or grain. They dug up yards to search for hidden food. They used special animals to sniff out any remaining food. The Party officials knew that if all the food were gone, the peasants would be dead. But they were still alive, so their must be hidden food. [143]

The peasants survived by eating roots. They boiled bark and their boot soles for soup broth. Some peasants in desperation started eating their dogs and cats. In response, the Party ordered village officials to bag a "certain quota of dog and cat skins" and went through the village shooting these animals to eliminate this source of food. The peasants began to eat birds and their eggs, and the communist activists organized bird hunts to eliminate that source. [144]

The terrible spring of 1932 was followed by the even worse spring of 1933. Vasily Grossman, a Soviet writer recorded: "When the snow melted true starvation began. People had swollen faces and legs and stomachs. They could not contain their urine...And now they ate anything at all. They caught mice, rats, sparrows, ants, earthworms. They ground up bones into flour, and did the same thing with leather and shoe soles; they cut up old skins and furs to make noodles of a kind and they cooked glue. And when the grass came up, they began to dig up the roots and ate the leaves and the buds, they used everything there was; dandelions, and burdocks and bluebells and willowroot, and sedums and nettles..." [145]

With nothing left, some of the peasants ate horse manure. Finally, some became cannibals and ate their own children, and the children of their neighbors that they could kidnap. [146]

The Famine of Ukraine & the Volga Colonies [147]

An eyewitness noted: "...*the fertile Ukrainian soil was covered with human corpses...I saw how special brigades gathered the corpses from the streets and houses, and carted them to common graves, or simply threw them in ravines.*"

The Italian Consul in Kharkov (300 miles west of the Volga River) reported that there was: "a growing commerce in human meat" and that people thru out countryside were killing and eating their own children. The Government distributed posters that read: 'EATING DEAD CHILDREN IS BARBARISM'. People knew that there was food in the cities and desperately tried to flee the countryside. In Kharkov in 1932, the police recovered 250 corpses every morning from the railway station.

Despite the enormous severity of the famine, the Government forbade doctors to put on death certificates that the cause of death was starvation. Because of this, the number of people who died during the famine cannot be accurately determined. It is estimated that between two and seven million people (Germans and Russians) died in Russia from this Stalin directed famine.[148]

Stalin achieved his goal and whole villages were now lifeless. Any that survived were too weak to think about independence or challenging the power of the Communist Party. Having decisively won, Stalin benevolently ended the quotas in March 1933. By April 1933, some army grain reserves were released for distribution to the dying peasants.[149]

The indigenous Russians and Ukrainian peasants that survived probably felt life improved somewhat after this famine. The records show that the Volga German colonies suffered a loss of between 15 to 20% of their population because of the famine. Much worse were the Ukrainian peasants with over 25% of their people dead. Stalin had beaten them, and so he left them alone.

Stalin was not finished with the German-Russians of the Volga. He was just warming up to his final solution - The Eradication and Genocide of the German-Russians.

Chapter 8
The End
Stalin's Plan

The rise to power in Germany of Hitler and his Nazi party worried Stalin about the loyalty of the Volga German-Russians. Some feel that this might be the reason for the purges of 1936 through 1938. However, all of Russia suffered from these purges, not just the Volga German-Russians.

By 1938, the Stalinist terror had slaughtered over 3 million people (including all of Stalin's rivals and their families). Russia had become crazy and paranoid, and the German language was forbidden except in the Volga region. Stalin did not trust the loyalty of the 300,000 Volga German-Russians deep in Russian territory, and quickly made plans for their immediate deportation after the wars' start. He needed some reason to "legitimize" his deportation plan. Within one month, the Soviet Government performed a series of large-scale "loyalty tests" in the Volga region.

In one test, a Soviet security police detachment, disguised as German soldiers, parachuted into the city of Engles to learn the peoples' response and determine if the German-Russians were loyal to Germany or to Russia. A few failed the test, and they were killed, but they found enough to give Stalin the "public" reason he needed for his plan.

That plan is explained in my following book:

"Moscow's Final Solution: The Genocide of the German-RussianVolga Colonies"

Summary

In spite of all horrible challenges that the Volga Germans were faced with they not only survived, but also prospered. They were so successful that they eventually became an embarrassment to the Russian Socialist Government. With the Government bearing down on them, the lucky ones left their Volga homeland for new lives in other areas. Those that stayed on were far less fortunate.

Forgotten Volga German Grave & Tombstone in Warenburg Cemetery 2003 [150]

We cannot forget all they did for us.

D. Philipp Kaiser 2014

Bibliography

Aid For Starving Russians, (The Nation, LVI 1892)

Ali, Tariq, *Trotsky For Beginners*,(Pantheon Books, New York, 1980)

American Relief to Russia, (American Review of Reviews, LIV 1892)

America to the starving people of Russia, Photo from the Hoover Institution Archives

American Volga Relief Society letters and documents, <http://www.nebraskahistory.org/lib-arch/research/treasures/volga_relief.htm>, accessed 11 April 2006

Another Child, <http://www.artukraine.com/famineart/famine10.htm>; accessed 10 April 2006

Bauer, Gottlieb, *Geschichte der deutschen Ansiedler an der Wolga*, (Sartov, Buchdruckerie "Energie", 1908)

Beratz, Gottlieb, *The German Colonies on the Lower Volga: Their Origin and Early Development*

(Lincoln, NE: American Historical Society of Germans from Russia, 1991)

Borovikovsky, Vladimir Lukich, *Catherine the Great*, 1794

Catherine the Great, <http://www.mnsu.edu/emuseum/history/russia/catherine.html>, accessed 11 April 2006

Child of Famine, <http://www.artukraine.com/famineart/famine10.htm>, accessed 10 April 2006

Conquest, Robert, *The Nation Killers: The Soviet Deportation of Nationalities,* (New York, NY: Macmillan Company, 1970)

Dobrinka, <http://dobrinka.wathenadesigns.com/>, accessed 9 April 2006

Don Cossacks, <http://www.infoplease.com/ce6/world/A0815851.html>, accessed 9 April 2006

Edgar, W, *Russia's Conflict With Hunger*, (American Review of Reviews, V, 1892)

Emelian Ivanovich Pugachev, <http://www.andrejkoymasky.com/ liv/fam/biop3/puga1.html>, accessed 25 June 2006

Emelian Ivanovich Pugachev, <http://www.infoplease.com/ce6/people/A0840478.html>, accessed 9 April 2006

Emilian Ivanovich Pugachev, <http://www.nndb.com/people/224/000069017/pugachev-cage. JPG>, accessed 9 April 2006

Families Fleeing, <http://www.volgagermans.net/volgagermans/images/Volga%20fam ine.jpg>, accessed 10 April 2006

Fisher, H.H., *The Famine in Soviet Russia 1919-1923*, (The McMillan Co, NY, 1927)

Freedom Promotes Wealth and Prosperity, <http://www.hawaii.edu/powerkills/WF.CHAP4.HTM>, accessed 28 Jun 2006

Geisinger, Adam, *From Catherine to Krushchev: The Story of Russia's Germans* (Winnipeg, Canada; Marian Press, 1974)

Geissler, Christian-Gottfried-Heinrich, *Kalmyks*, illustration by German graphic artist and engraver, (1770-1844)

Geschichte der Russlanddeutschen , <http://www.russlanddeutschegeschichte.de>, accessed 10 April 2006

Gift of the American people, Photo from the Hoover Institution Archives

Golder, Frank & Hutchinson, Lincoln, *On the Trail of the Russian Famine,* (Stanford Univ Press, 127)

Great Famine,
<http://en.wikipedia.org/wiki/Great_Famine_of_1315-1317>, accessed 11 April 2006

Harms, Wilmer A., *Insights Into Russia,* (Journal of the AHSGR, Lincoln, NE, Volume 26, No. 2 Spring 2003)

Haynes, Emma S., *A History of the Volga Relief Society,* (AHSGR, Lincoln, NE, 1982)

History of Kalmykia,
<http://www.zum.de/whklma/histatlas/russia/haxkalmykia.html>, accessed 28 June 2006

History of Russia,
<http://www.teach12.com/ttc/Assets/courseDescriptions/8380.asp?pc=SiteIndex>, accessed 8 April 2006

History of Russia's Germans,
<http://www.russlanddeutschegeschichte.de/englisch1/luebeck_oranienbaum.htm>, accessed 8 April 2006

Kalmykia, <http://www.answers.com/topic/kalmykia>, accessed 11 April 2006

Kessler, Bishop Joseph, *Knights Of Columbus Hall Speech*, (Ellis County News, Kansas- Thursday, February 9, 1922)

Kipchaks, <http://en.wikipedia.org/wiki/Kipchak>, accessed 12 April 2006

Kirghiz, http://www.1911encyclopedia.org/K/KI/KIRGHIZ.htm, accessed 28 June 2006

Lords and Peasants,
<http://www.history.ucsb.edu/syllabi/fall05/Hasegawa/Lecture18Peasants.pdf>, accessed 12 April 2006

Mai, Brent Alan & Reeves-Marquardt, Dona, *German Migration to the Russian Volga (1764-1767)*, (AHSGR, Lincoln, NE, 2003)

Mai, Brent Alan, *Transport of the Volga Germans from Oranienbaum to the Colonies on the Volga 1766-1767*, AHSGR, Lincoln, NE, 1998)

Maier, Rev Carl, *A Pilgrimage of Two Hundred Years*, (70th Anniversary of the Free Evangelical Lutheran Cross Church, Fresno, CA. 1962)

Matthaei, Friedrich, *Die deutschen Ansiedlungen in Russland*, (Leipzig, H.Fries, 1866)

Medieval Warm Period, <http://en.wikipedia.org/wiki/Medieval_Warm_Period>, accessed 12 April 2006

Miller, Patrice, *Volga Germans*, <http://www.webbitt.com/volga>, accessed 11 April 2006

Moving the Bodies, <http://www.artukraine.com/famineart/famine10.htm>, accessed 10 April 2006

Packet Boats, <http://www.postalheritage.org.uk/history/transport/water_packetboats.html>, accessed 15 July 2005

Perov, Vasily. *Pugachev's Judgement.* 1875. Oil on canvas, 150x238 cm. The History Museum, Moscow, Russia

Pfeifer, Leona, *The Life of the German Woman in Russia*, (Journal of the American Historical Society of Germans from Russia, Lincoln, NE, Volume 26, No. 2 Spring 2003)

Pleve, Igor R., *The German Colonies on the Volga: The Second Half of the Eighteenth Century*, (AHSGR, Lincoln, NE, 2001)

Pugachev, <http://www.corvalliscommunitypages.com/images_sounds/pugachev_2.jpg>, accessed 9 April 2006

Pugachev, <http://www.eefy.editme.com/Pugachev>, accessed 27 June 2006

Pushkin, Alexander, *The History of Pugachev*, (Phoenix Press, London, 2001)

Ransome, Arthur, *Famine on the Volga*, (The Guardian, London, October 11, 1921)

Roll, Mitch, *German-Russian Volga Area Map*, (Dallas, Texas)

Russians in Exile, <http://www.joebattsarm.com/lexicografie/dias9.html>, accessed 12 April 2006

Saul, Norman, *Concord and Conflict, The United States and Russia, 1867-1914*, pp. 335-355

Schreiber, Steven, *Volga Relief Society*, <http://www.volgagermans.net/volgagermans/Volga%20Relief%20 Society>, accessed 5 May 2005

Schwabenland, Emma, *A History of the Volga Relief Society* (AHSGR, Lincoln, NE, 1982)

Sinner, Samuel D., *The Open Wound - The Genocide of German Ethnic Minorities In Russia and the Soviet Union, 1915-1949---And Beyond*, (Germans From Russia Collection, North Dakota State University Libraries, Fargo, North Dakota, 2000)

Starvation is Worse Fyrther into Provinces – Death List in Communities Greater as One Proceeds up Volga River, (Daily Pioneer, Mandan, North Dakota, November 9, 1921)

Stradling, J. and Reason, W., *In the Land of Tolstoi* (London James Clarke and Company, 1897)

Stumpp, Karl, *Emigration from Germany to Russia from 1763 to 1786*, (AHSGR, Lincoln, NE 2001)

The European Theater, <http://www.frob.net/syw05/history.html>, 12 August 2005

The Great Famine – Genocide in Soviet Ukraine, 1932-33, <http://www.artukraine.com/famineart/famine14.htm>, accessed 11 April 2006

The Volga Germans, A Brief History <http://www.lhm.org/LID/lidhist.htm>, accessed 10 April 2006

Tolstoy, M. de Courcel, *The Ultimate Reconciliation* (New York Charles Scribner's Sons, 1988)

Uprising in Warenburg, <http://www.volgagermans.net/warenburg/Warenburg_Uprising.htm>, accessed 10 April 2006

Volga Famine of 1921-22, <http://www.volgagermans.net/volgagermans/images/Volga famine.jpg>, accessed 10 April 2006

Watson, Fiona, *One hundred years of famine - a pause for reflection*, <http://www.ennonline.net/fex/08/ms20.html>, accessed 10 April 2006

Webster's Ninth New Collegiate Dictionary, (Merriam-Webster, Springfield, MA, 1984)

White, Sharon, *German Tombstone in Warenburg Cemetery in 2003*

Williams, Hattie Plum, *The Czar's Germans*, (AHSGR, Lincoln, NE, 1975)

Wucher, Albert, *Illustrierte Weltgeschichte*, (Linden Verlag, Koln, 1982)

Yemelyan Pugachev, <http://en.wikipedia.org/wiki/Yemelyan_Pugachev>, accessed 28 June 2006

Züge, Gottlieb, *The Russian Colonist or Christian Gottlieb Züge's Life in Russia with a Description of Russian Life and Habits in Their Asiatic Provinces* (Germany 1802)

End Notes

[1] Author created

[2] Williams, Hattie Plum, *The Czar's Germans*, p. 106

[3] Pleve, Igor R., *The German Colonies on the Volga: The Second Half of the Eighteenth Century*, p.106

[4] Bauer, Gottlieb, *Geschichte der deutschen Ansiedler an der Wolga*, p.19

[5] Williams, Hattie Plum, *The Czar's Germans*, p. 56

[6] *Packet Boats*

[7] Williams, Hattie Plum, *The Czar's Germans*, p. 56

[8] *History of Russia's Germans*

[9] Williams, Hattie Plum., *The Czar's Germans*, p. 107

[10] Geisinger, Adam, *From Catherine to Krushchev: The Story of Russia's Germans,* p. 10

[11] *Geschichte der Russlanddeutschen*

[12] ibid

[13] Beratz, Gottlieb, *The German Colonies on the Lower Volga*, pp. 50-51

[14] ibid

[15] Haynes, Emma S., *A History of the Volga Relief Society*, p.17

[16] Beratz, Gottlieb, *The German Colonies on the Lower Volga*, pp. 51, 54

[17] ibid, p. 55

[18] ibid

[19] Author created

[20] *Geschichte der Russlanddeutschen*

[21] Roll, Mitch, *German-Russian Volga Area Map*

[22] Miller, Patrice, *Volga Germans*

[23] Photographer unknown

[24] Geisinger, Adam, *From Catherine to Krushchev: The Story of Russia's Germans,* p. 15

[25] Williams, Hattie Plum., *The Czar's Germans*, p. 111

[26] Haynes, Emma S., *A History of the Volga Relief Society*, p.17

[27] Züge, Gottlieb, *The Russian Colonist or Christian*

Gottlieb Züge's Life in Russia
[28] Haynes, Emma S., *A History of the Volga Relief Society*, p.17
[29] Pfeifer, Leona, *The Life of the German Woman in Russia*, p.21
[30] Mai, Brent Allen, *Transport of the Volga Germans from Oranienbaum to the Colonies on the Volga*
[31] Mai, Brent Alan; Reeves-Marquardt, Dona, *German Migration to the Russian Volga (1764-1767)*, p. iii
[32] Pfeifer, Leona, *The Life of the German Woman in Russia*, p.21
[33] Beratz, Gottlieb, *The German Colonies on the Lower Volga*, p. 80
[34] ibid, p. 81
[35] ibid, p. 80
[36] Author created
[37] Beratz, Gottlieb, *The German Colonies on the Lower Volga*, p. 138
[38] ibid, p. 129
[39] ibid
[40] ibid, pp. 129-130
[41] ibid, p. 130
[42] Author created
[43] ibid, p.11
[44] Maier, Rev Carl, *A Pilgrimage of Two Hundred Years*, pp. 5-15
[45] Harms, Wilmer A., *Insights Into Russia*, p.15
[46] Geisinger, Adam, *From Catherine to Krushchev: The Story of Russia's Germans*, p. 5
[47] Haynes, Emma S., *A History of the Volga Relief Society* , p. 13
[48] ibid, p. 16
[49] Stumpp, Karl, *Emigration from Germany to Russia from 1763 to 1786*
[50] Wucher, Albert, *Illustrierte Weltgeschichte*, pp. 762-764
[51] *The European Theater*
[52] Stumpp, Karl, *Emigration from Germany to Russia from 1763 to 1862*, p. 25
[53] Borovikovsky, Vladimir Lukich, *Catherine the Great*, 1794
[54] ibid
[55] Photographer unknown

[56] Author created

[57] Beratz, Gottlieb, *The German Colonies on the Lower Volga*, p. 329

[58] *Kirghiz*, http://www.1911encyclopedia.org/K/KI/KIRGHIZ.htm

[59] Artist unknown

[60] Haynes, Emma S., *A History of the Volga Relief Society*, p.19

[61] Author created

[62] Matthaei, Friedrich, *Die deutschen Ansiedlungen in Russland*, p.127

[63] Pleve, Igor R., *The German Colonies on the Volga*, p. 183

[64] *History of Kalmykia*

[65] *Kalmykia*

[66] Haynes, Emma S., *A History of the Volga Relief Society*, p.19

[67] Geissler, Christian-Gottfried-Heinrich, ***Kalmyks***

[68] *Pugachev*, http://www.eefy.editme.com/Pugachev

[69] *Yemelyan Pugachev*

[70] *Don Cossacks*

[71] *Pugachev*, http://www.eefy.editme.com/Pugachev

[72] *ibid*

[73] *Lords and Peasants*

[74] *Yemelyan Pugachev*

[75] *History of Russia*

[76] *Pugachev*, http://www.eefy.editme.com/Pugachev

[77] *ibid*

[78] *Pugachev*, http://www.corvalliscommunitypages.com/images_sounds/pugachev_2.jpg

[79] *Emelian Ivanovich Pugachev*

[80] Author created

[81] *Catherine the Great*

[82] Geisinger, Adam, *From Catherine to Krushchev: The Story of Russia's Germans*, p. 19

[83] *Emilian Ivanovich Pugachev*, pugachev-cage.JPG

[84] *Emilian Pugachev*

[85] *Emelian Ivanovich Pugachev*, http://www.andrejkoymasky.com/

liv/fam/biop3/puga1.html

[86] Pushkin, Alexander, *The History of Pugachev*

[87] *Yemelyan Pugachev*

[88] Perov, Vasily, *Pugachev's Judgement,* 1875

[89] Kessler, Bishop Joseph, *Knights Of Columbus Hall Speech,*

[90] Conquest, Robert, *The Nation Killers: The Soviet Deportation of Nationalities,* p. 260

[91] Schreiber, Steven, *Volga Relief Society*

[92] Haynes, Emma S., *A History of the Volga Relief Society*, p.28

[93] Sinner, Samuel D., *The Open Wound - The Genocide of German Ethnic Minorities In Russia,* pp.18 -19

[94] *Dobrinka*

[95] Sinner, Samuel D., *The Open Wound - The Genocide of German Ethnic Minorities In Russia,* pp.18 -19

[96] *Uprising in Warenburg*

[97] Sinner, Samuel D., *The Open Wound - The Genocide of German Ethnic Minorities In Russia,* pp.18 -19

[98] *Webster's Ninth New Collegiate Dictionary,* p. 448

[99] *Great Famine*

[100] *Medieval Warm Period*

[101] *Great Famine*

[102] Stradling, J. and Reason, W., *In the Land of Tolstoi,* p. 45

[103] Tolstoy, M. de Courcel, *The Ultimate Reconciliation,* p. 22

[104] Stradling, J. and Reason, W., *In the Land of Tolstoi,* p. 59

[105] *Aid For Starving Russians,* p. 130

[106] *American Relief to Russia,* p. 267

[107] Edgar, W, *Russia's Conflict With Hunger,* p. 693

[108] ibid

[109] Saul, Norman, *Concord and Conflict, The United States and Russia, 1867-1914,* pp. 335-355

[110] Schreiber, Steven, *Volga Relief Society*

[111] *The Volga Germans, A Brief History*

[112] Geisinger, Adam, *From Catherine to Krushchev: The Story of Russia's Germans,* p. 243

[113] *Volga Famine of 1921-22*

[114] ibid

[115] Schreiber, Steven, *Volga Relief Society*

[116] *Russians in Exile*

[117] *Moving the Bodies*

[118] Author created

[119] *Child of Famine*

[120] Ransome, Arthur, *Famine on the Volga*

[121] *Another Child*

[122] ibid, *To The Food Lines*

[123] *Families Fleeing*

[124] *Starvation is Worse Fyrther into Provinces – Death List in Communities Greater as One Proceeds*

[125] Golder, Frank & Hutchinson, Lincoln, *On the Trail of the Russian Famine*, p. 88

[126] Schreiber, Steven, *Volga Relief Society*

[127] Schwabenland, Emma, *A History of the Volga Relief Society*, pp. 39-42

[128] ibid

[129] Fisher, H.H., *The Famine in Soviet Russia 1919-1923*, p 556

[130] Schwabenland, Emma, *A History of the Volga Relief Society*, pp. 39-42

[131] *America to the starving people of Russia*

[132] *Gift of the American people*

[133] *American Volga Relief Society letters and documents*

[134] Ali, Tariq, *Trotsky for Beginners*, pp. 109-111

[135] Conquest, Robert, *The Nation Killers: The Soviet Deportation of Nationalities*, p. 260.

[136] Harms, Wilmer A., *Insights Into Russia*, p.16

[137] Watson, Fiona, *One hundred years of famine - a pause for reflection*

[138] *The Great Famine – Genocide in Soviet Ukraine, 1932-33*

[139] Watson, Fiona, *One hundred years of famine - a pause for reflection*

[140] *The Great Famine – Genocide in Soviet Ukraine, 1932-33*

[141] *Freedom Promotes Wealth and Prosperity*

[142] *ibid*

[143] *ibid*

[144] *ibid*

[145] Watson, Fiona, *One hundred years of famine - a pause for reflection*

[146] *Freedom Promotes Wealth and Prosperity*

[147] Author created

[148] Watson, Fiona, *One hundred years of famine - a pause for reflection*

[149] *Freedom Promotes Wealth and Prosperity*

[150] White, Sharon, *German Tombstone in Warenburg Cemetery in 2003*